SALVATION'S SONG

'Many have written books about worship, emphasising the need for it to be the first priority in our lives, but Marcus goes much further than that. Always one for an original take on things, he leads us on an exploration of the 'big picture', demonstrating how all the important themes of the Bible (such as sin, redemption and the cross) are primarily worship issues - sin is first and foremost wrong worship, and Jesus' death on the cross is perfect worship. I found it original and extremely stimulating.'

Philip Lawson Johnston

'What a wonderful stimulus to think seriously and creatively about worship! Marcus Green has done us all a service with this wonderful book. It deserves to be read by all thinking about the place of worship in the lives of individuals and churches.'

Alister McGrath, Wycliffe Hall, Oxford

'This is a liberating and exciting book, which has the potential to open up some very new channels in mission. Marcus Green writes out of a tough and varied pastoral experience, with consummate skills in exegesis as well as a fine ear for the particular human stories woven in to his theology.'

Archbishop Rowan Williams

'*Salvation's Song* is a great book. A thought-provoking read that lays down an essential challenge to recapture the big picture of worship. I've been hugely inspired and convicted as I've delved into this book. I'd encourage all to read it.'

Tim Hughes

Salvation's Song

MARCUS GREEN

survivor

Unless otherwise indicated, biblical quotations are
from the New International Version © 1973, 1978, 1984
by the International Bible Society.

ISBN 1 84291 178 3

Published by
KINGSWAY COMMUNICATIONS LTD
Lottbridge Drove, Eastbourne BN23 6NT, England.
Email: books@kingsway.co.uk

Book design and production for the publishers by
Bookprint Creative Services, P.O. Box 827, BN21 3YJ, England.
Printed in Great Britain.

Contents

Acknowledgements   7
Foreword by Matt Redman   11
Foreword by Mike Pilavachi   15
Why Another Book on Worship?   17

Part One: Worship and the Gospel
1. Another Fine Mess   27
2. Perfect Worship – the Cross   45
3. Jesus Is Lord: So What?   63
4. Free at Last   86

Part Two: Worshipping Jesus
Interlude: The Kiss of Worship   113
5. O Worship the King   119
6. More Than a Song   142
7. Tell Me the Stories of Jesus   165
8. The Big Picture   203

Appendix: The Worship Word   241

Acknowledgements

Thank you to everyone who helped with any part of this whole project! It is hard to isolate individuals, because so many people have offered time and opinions to contribute to my work, but here are a few of the many. First, thanks to Bishop Graham Cray, for his wisdom, patience and guidance as I worked through all of this, and indeed to all the staff and students at Ridley Hall, Cambridge, back in 1999–2000, especially 'F' staircase, for welcoming me into their community as I researched, read, thought things through, changed my mind and needed sounding boards for every latest idea.

A particular debt of gratitude belongs to Archbishop Rowan Williams, the Revd Paul Thompson, Dr Neil Smith and Phil Lawson Johnston for the time and thought put into their contributions, which appear in Chapter 7; it was cheeky of me to ask for your help, and gracious of you to give it. Thanks too to Chris and Ruth

Holmwood, Katy Walton and Lindsay Jack, for bringing to my attention spelling, grammatical and theological errors; they take much credit for many details.

A very big thank you to the many people who helped share the financial and prayer burdens of my taking time out from parish ministry to write this book: Bishop Huw Jones; members of St Michael's, Aberystwyth, St Aldate's, Oxford, and St Barnabas, Cambridge; Catharine Morris; James Nickols; Nigel and Angela Bamping; Gill Walker; Pauline Baker; John Walker; the Isla Johnston Trust; Bill and Fiona Broadhurst . . . space does not permit me to go on, so forgive me if I have not included your name here.

Thanks to Mum, Dad and Lorna, and Gill and Ben for being family: I am grateful for everything you have given me. Thanks to wise heads who heard early thoughts and made me work harder on them – David Bryan and Dick France in particular. Thanks to Joan and Robin Church, for the use of their flat, and for the haven that it was during the writing process – particularly the garden in the summer! Charlie (the dog) enjoyed it no end.

Ah yes, Charlie the dog – much missed and much loved. He taught me much about what it means to be unconditionally loved. Now his successor, Matt, fulfils the same role, and has listened patiently to various rewrites as I have tried them out first on him.

Thanks to Mike Pilavachi, who has been instrumental both in the ideas and the actual publishing of this, as well as to all at Survivor Books and Kingsway; and to

Matt Redman, for his generous foreword. Thanks too to Richard Herkes, for staying excited by this book and for not giving up!

Thank you to all who have over the last 20 years made me value worshipping Jesus: friends, colleagues, pastors and teachers. You have shaped me, and therefore this book, more than you know, and I am grateful for it.

Foreword

by Matt Redman

Last week I came across a picture book called *Powers of Ten* (based on the film by Charles and Ray Eames). It's a pretty incredible thing. It starts out looking at a view ten million light years across – and there, right in the middle of the page, seen as only a tiny speck, is the Milky Way. Then every page zooms in by the power of ten. We pass right through the Milky Way, through the spiral patterns of the galaxy, zooming in towards our solar system. Before long we're headed straight for the earth, zooming in on the city of Chicago, and a particular park there. Focusing in on a man lying on a picnic blanket, the images keep moving in by the power of ten, and we journey beneath the surface of the skin, right into his DNA – and eventually see just a single proton.

The *Powers of Ten* picture book shows the big picture, and then takes us on a fascinating journey right into the detail. Marcus Green's book does exactly the same. Marcus starts off by giving us the big picture about worship – what it is and what it isn't. Then in every chapter he zooms in and teaches us about worship in greater detail. Part Two of the book focuses right in on Matthew's gospel, and from there moves in even further to highlight ten stories or parables that educate us about true worship. It's a refreshing way to learn.

There are two types of clever people in this world. The first type knows a whole lot of complicated stuff, but unfortunately has no clue how to unravel it for public consumption. The second kind of person is just as learned, yet somehow finds word pictures and analogies to communicate these grand truths simply to someone like me. Marcus is undoubtedly a clever man, and thankfully for us, he falls into the latter category! He has a real gift of delving deeper, bringing valuable worship insights out of Bible passages we might have read many times before. Perhaps the most striking of these are Marcus's comments on Jesus as the perfect worshipper, and the cross as the ultimate act of worship. Within the context of Jesus as 'Lord' (and much time is spent refreshing our understanding of that word), Marcus focuses in on just how powerful and perfect an act of worship Jesus offered up to the Father at the cross. As I journeyed through his comments on Psalm 22, and the words Jesus cried out at the cross from the songbook of Israel, they did more than just educate my mind – they led my heart to worship.

This book helps us to 'worship with understanding' –

an essential thing for the singing church today. We worship with passion and enthusiasm, and rightly so. But it's vital that we also worship with understanding – gaining a grander view of the God we worship, and a greater grasp of all he requires and desires from us. *Salvation's Song* does just that – inviting us into the big picture of worship.

I hope Marcus's writing truly leads you in worship, as it did me.

Foreword
by Mike Pilavachi

This is a significant and timely book. It arrives at a time when the 'worship debate' is warming up. Some of us have been immersed in the practical aspects of worship with music and have been thinking about and experimenting with all sorts of styles, raising questions from 'Is it anointed?' and 'Is it culturally relevant?' to the base question of 'Is it working?' Until recently, we have perhaps not done as much theological study and reflection as we should. Others have seen the gaps in our theology and as a result sometimes a superficiality in our practice and have asked questions like 'What is worship?', 'Should we ever call singing worship?' and 'Is worship as a gathered community more about the horizontal dimension (singing and speaking truth to one another) than it is about the vertical (bringing an offering to God)?'

Salvation's Song is significant and timely because it

addresses all these issues and goes even deeper, finding worship at the very heart of Christian faith. This book is great theology. It is first of all thoroughly biblical and is fresh and original. There are golden nuggets of revelation that have drawn me deeper into informed worship. Marcus opened up some familiar scriptures in such a way that my first reaction was 'eureka' and the second was 'Why didn't I see that?'

In this book we see the 'big picture' and the picture is gloriously, wonderfully big! Worship is a way of life and our ultimate model is Jesus who is revealed as the perfect worshipper as well as the perfect Saviour. I had never seen Calvary as perfect worship before.

Marcus's book is not written from a distant ivory tower but rather it is theology with passion. Marcus is a theologian with a pastor's heart. As a worship leader he is a practitioner. He loves God, loves theology, loves worship and loves God's people. Above all it is this combination that makes Salvation's Song unique. This is brilliant stuff. I warmly recommend it.

Why Another Book
on Worship?

I was sitting in Starbuck's coffee house in Cambridge, having a drink with a friend from Ridley Hall. Rupert and I sometimes went there to talk through biblical issues so we could learn from each other. On this particular occasion, our conversation took a sudden swerve when Rupert asked simply, 'So, what would you say the gospel *is*?'

You see, I'd finished my second curacy in Wales to spend a year in Cambridge writing a book on worship. And whenever I said that to people, I normally observed one of two reactions: either their eyes would glaze over, because they thought I meant I was writing a book on singing, or they would get very excited, because they thought I meant I was writing a book on singing! Then as I explained to both groups of people that this was not what I was trying to do, some would stay excited while others glazed over even more. But Rupert had got to the heart of what I was about. And in answer to his question I replied, 'I think the gospel is "We can worship God".'

It's a bit like a kettle boiling. You can see a kettle boiling and you ask two bystanders why it is doing so. They give you two very different answers. The first person talks of the technicalities involved in making the kettle boil: the plug is in the socket, the power is switched on and electricity is racing through the wiring in order to heat the filament in the kettle, which in turn is heating the water, and as the water reaches the right temperature – hey presto, the kettle boils. You then ask the second person why the kettle is boiling, and she replies, 'Because I want a cup of tea.' Both answers are correct. But they are making different points.

Now when I say the gospel is 'We can worship God', I am in no way arguing with those who say that it is really all about justification by grace through faith. I believe that. I just think it's the technical answer: how the gospel works, the electricity answer to my kettle question. And I have this sneaky suspicion that the answer most people want – and really the answer most people *know* – is the cup of tea answer: the answer that makes sense practically, the answer that makes a difference. That's my answer. Because if I say that at the end of the day worshipping God is what the Christian life is all about, most people agree. It is 'the chief end of man', in the words of the Westminster Shorter Catechism. Now if that is true, and worship is the big picture – the bottom line, the *sine qua non* of

Christianity – then worship should be at the heart of all our theologising. But so often I try to read big books about God, don't get a whiff of worship, and end up feeling as if I've learned a lot about doctrines like sin and salvation only I'm sure there must be more. I want to see worship throughout the Bible, and I am convinced that there must be more to it than stories of Paul and Silas singing in jail. Worship *is* the big picture. Let's see it as such.

So my aim in this book is to begin to place our worship of God in this larger context. I'm not writing a book about the way I *do* worship, and how I see the practice of worship demonstrated in the Bible. There are many excellent books that do that sort of thing already. Instead, I want to take a step sideways, and see how the issue of worship affects some of the major ideas of our Christian faith. Along the way I might throw in a few posers for you to think about, such as how such an understanding might question or deepen some of our practices.

So what *is* worship?

Ah, what a good question. And I guess if you are going to read a book that aims to put worship at the heart of our faith, you have a right to know what I mean by worship, because different people will give you different answers. In my experience, most people's ideas tend towards one of three categories.

First, there is the intellectual approach, which

describes worship as a state of mind, an abstract concept, if you will. Peter Shaffer in *Equus* says, 'Without worship, you shrink; it's as brutal as that.'[1] This emphasis is very good at picking up the idea that worship is of the greatest importance. Christopher Cocksworth captures something of the force of this viewpoint:

> Worship is like the great cheer echoing around a football stadium as the critical goal is scored. Like the roar of the crowd, worship tells us that something has happened which has made a difference to the way things are. And as we listen to the chant, we can tell who scored the goal.[2]

People who focus on this fairly cerebral understanding of worship often pick up on the origins of our English word 'worship', deriving it from a Saxon word, *weorthscipe*; they talk about the nature of worth and value, and see worship as something that finds ultimate value in God. Some go on to see that in the relationship of worship, we give worth to God, and in the process receive worth from him. There is a very attractive flow here, a dynamic relationship between us and God, a two-way stream of love that many of us want to affirm. When we worship, when we give ourselves to him, we do also receive from God. Of course, this is all very abstract – we like the ideas, but we still don't know what it is we are *doing*! How do we actually walk down this two-way street?

Some react to this vagueness by placing worship firmly in the context of Sunday church gatherings. Worship is an act in which we sing, express our love and our loyalty, engage with God and touch the divine and are touched by it. We may worship individually, but the corporate is most people's norm. John Wimber, in talking about the priorities of his Vineyard movement, which delights in prolonged musical worship, defined worship as 'the act of freely loving God, responding to him with awe, submission and respect'.[3] Worship is an act, something we do. Karl Barth would agree with him: 'Christian worship is the most momentous, the most urgent, the most glorious act that can take place in human life.'[4] Well, we liked the ideas of the first definition, but we all know the experience of this one. Taking time week by week to worship Jesus is our common Christian life, and though often it seems weak and poor, sometimes the sense of the presence of God is powerful and transforming. There is something about the power of music in worship. Luther himself wrote, 'My heart bubbles up and overflows in response to music, which has so often refreshed me and delivered me from dire plagues.'[5]

3. John Wimber, 'Worship: Intimacy with God' in *Worship and Revival Songs and Essays* (Vineyard, 1995), p. 222.
4. Karl Barth, quoted in J. von Allmen, *Worship: Its Theology and Practice* (Lutterworth, 1965), p. 133.
5. Quoted in Roland Bainton, *Here I Stand* (Lion, 1978), p. 341.

Of course, there are also those who, either because
they are totally unmusical or because they have a more
practical and less romantic nature, find this emphasis on
the experience of public worship to be unsatisfactory.
Some want to emphasise that for worship to be valid, it
must have a practical impact on our everyday living.
Others take that idea a bit further, and say that the way
we lead our everyday lives is the evidence of worship.
The corporate act is not worship – it is about building
one another up, about teaching and learning the word
of God, about prayer and giving. Worship is lifestyle. We
are taken back to the *weorthscipe* word, and reminded
that worship is about what we value: serving God.
Worship teaches us that we are God's servants, ready to
do his will, and acts of obedience are the truest worship,
free from feelings and the risk of emotional frothiness.

Now I agree with all three of these definitions of
worship. I do not see them as being in any way set
against each other; rather, they complement and
complete each other. Worship is a state of mind – or,
perhaps better, an attitude of the heart. We must have a
right relationship with the Lord of all things, which
means that worshipping God comes before anything
else. It is the highest calling. But worship must also be
expressed in corporate songs and prayers and liturgies
of heart and voice. We need time to say to God how we
feel, how we want to feel, how we understand his truth,
and how we need him to meet us and make those
truths a deeper reality for us. We are the body of Christ;
we have to say these things together. We have to wait

on our Lord together. We have to celebrate and mourn and feast and fast together. And then we live out our worship day by day. The words on our lips only have meaning if the acts of our lives match up to them. So we say we will obey God; then we go out and do it. The doing is as much worship as the singing; the singing is as much worship as the doing: and one without the other is only half the story. Archbishop William Temple adds all these ideas together in this way:

> To worship is to quicken the conscience by the holiness of God; to feed the mind with the truth of God; to purge the imagination by the beauty of God; to open the heart to the love of God; and to devote the will to the purpose of God.[6]

So what is my definition of worship? Worship forms the whole Godward response of our lives, focused and expressed as we gather together to sing God's praise. Worship is the way we lead lives of thankfulness to God, demonstrating his power and his love and our daily commitment to him, but worship is most clearly expressed in our songs, prayers and silences as we meet together on the Lord's day. We are made to worship God.

As you read this book, I hope you will begin to see this is where I come from, this is how I understand worship, this is what I am talking about. Perhaps two

---

6. Quoted in Mike Pilavachi, *For the Audience of One* (Hodder & Stoughton, 1999), p. 140.

bits of liturgy from the Church of England's now defunct *Alternative Service Book* will serve as useful reminders. The first comes from the beginning of Morning Prayer, as we hear why we have come together; the second comes from the end of the Communion service, as we prepare to leave the place of worship to continue our lives of service.

We have come together as the family of God in our Father's presence
to offer him praise and thanksgiving,
to hear and receive his holy word,
to bring before him the needs of the world,
to ask his forgiveness of our sins,
and to seek his grace
that through his Son Jesus Christ
we may give ourselves to his service.

Almighty God,
we thank you for feeding us
with the body and blood of your dear Son Jesus Christ.
Through him we offer you our souls and bodies
to be a living sacrifice.
Send us out in the power of your Spirit
to live and work
to your praise and glory. Amen.

PART ONE:

WORSHIP
AND THE GOSPEL

1

Another Fine Mess

I t was a bad start to the day. My car was booked in for a service first thing in the morning, and I needed to be back home pretty soon after leaving it, so I had asked a friend with a Landrover to drop my bike over by the garage the night before. That way I could easily cycle into town despite the rush hour traffic and get to my next appointment. The only problem was that overnight somebody had tried to steal the bike, and finding the lock too good for them, they had settled on vandalising the back wheel, leaving it totally wrecked. So I was stuck on the wrong side of town with a broken bike and a bad temper, wondering why anybody would do such a thing.

The chap in the repair shop said he saw four or five bikes a week like that. And it was only a dumb bike – not a friend who'd been mugged or a nation wiped off the face of the earth! But it upset me. It wouldn't happen in a perfect world.

But that's the point, isn't it? This is not a perfect world. It's a world with bike vandals, rush hour traffic, toxic waste, cancer, grief and a million and one other things we hate. So what has gone wrong? Who or what is to blame for this and every other fine mess we find ourselves having to face – or is this the way God meant life to be?

Now bear with me. I know you thought you were reading a book on worship, and suddenly I'm having a whinge and confronting you with the evils of contemporary society. I bet you can just see an evangelistic tract on sin and redemption coming at you. But given that as Christians we are agreed the problem with the world is sin, have you ever stopped to think about what sin is, where it comes from, how it has the effect it has? And have you ever considered sin as a worship issue? Because if worship is the big picture in life, then it has to say things about the big issues that face us in our lives. Like sin.

The first command

The problem is that most of us come into contact with so much sin that we miss the big picture. Whether it is the sins we suffer at the hands of others (like the damage done to my poor bicycle) or the sins we inflict upon ourselves (like greed or lust or those thought patterns we never acknowledge to anyone else), there are just so many of these little things to clog our mind's eye that we can't see beyond them. Oh, if we are feeling righteous or if we are truly altruistic we might just see as far as genocide in the Balkans or the exploitation of child labour in the Far East. But Jesus sets us a different agenda, and it might do us good to think about what he has to say on the question.

Hearing that Jesus had silenced the Sadducees, the Pharisees got together. One of them, an expert in the law, tested him with this question: 'Teacher, which is the greatest commandment in the Law?' Jesus replied: ' "Love the Lord your God with all your heart and with all your soul and with all your mind." This is the first and greatest commandment. And the second is like it: "Love your neighbour as yourself." All the Law and the Prophets hang on these two commandments.' (Matthew 22:34–40)

Now you have to wonder what the Pharisees were on. They have heard that Jesus silenced the Sadducees, who were not dull – though they were no real friends of the Pharisees. And if Jesus has just done that to these guys, it hardly seems a good idea to have a go at him, does it? But one of them, a real expert, fancies his chances. I suppose if he comes out of it well, the Sadducees will look bad by comparison. So this guy asks his question: 'Which is the greatest commandment in the Law?'

Jesus replies using Moses' summary of the Law in Deuteronomy chapter 6. In chapter 5 Moses has restated the Ten Commandments for everyone to hear, and then he goes on to encourage them to keep the laws of God so that they might receive the blessings God has for them. The summary Jesus quotes is part of that encouragement. In essence, he says, the most important thing is to love God. This is the beginning and the heart of the whole Law of God. It sums up the first four of the Ten Commandments: serve the Lord only, make no idols, don't blaspheme and keep a Sabbath to worship God. The Law begins with rules for worship:

- Worship is about serving God alone, not having anything else in life that takes his place, keeping him as number one. This is the first commandment.
- Worship is about the God who made us, so don't get confused into somehow thinking that we should serve the things we make – that is a nonsense. This is the second commandment.
- Worship is about the name of the Lord, and words are important, so do not misuse the holy or call holy anything that is not. This is the third commandment.
- Worship is about the whole of life, so throughout the whole of life take regular time out to remember the Lord and what he has done for us: the fourth commandment.

In other words, says Moses, and says Jesus quoting Moses, worship is about loving God with everything you have and are. And it comes first. Everything else comes from it.

Perhaps your idea of the Law in the Old Testament, the Law the Jews had to keep, is that it is a moral code –

don't do this, do do that. So it is. I'm not about to deny that. But the moral code comes from worshipping God first. The way we deal with each other is a result of worshipping God. If we love him and learn from him, taking on his standards as we come before him, then we will live lives of moral excellence. It works like this: if we worship a God who cares for us, we will care for others; if we worship a God of faithfulness, we will be faithful in all our relationships; if we worship a God of truth, we will be a truthful people. Right worship leads to right lifestyle. But right worship must come first. It is the first commandment. The stuff about loving neighbours comes second because it only comes as a subsidiary, a follow-on to the first.

So what is sin all about? Breaking God's Law? Yes. But what is the greatest – and by that I mean the root, the basic, the first and causal – commandment? To love God and worship him. So what is the greatest – the root, the basic, the first and causal – sin? To not love God and not worship him. All the Law and the prophets hang on loving God; all the sin in the world hangs on not loving him.

Sin is a worship issue. If everybody loved God and worshipped him as an expression of that love, then my bike would not have had to go to the repair shop. If everybody had always loved God and worshipped him the whole world would be different: there would be no hospitals, because there would be nobody suffering or in pain, because there would never have been any sin. There is no sickness in a perfect world. Great human disasters like the Holocaust would not have happened. Closer to home, you wouldn't hate your job. I wouldn't envy you for earning more than I do. Next door wouldn't gossip about us. There would be no war if we all loved and worshipped God with all our heart and mind and soul.

But sin is about not worshipping God, not loving him, not putting him first. So there is war. And all the rest. And the problem is not that because we do not worship God, we do not worship at all – leaving sin to fill the vacuum (as if all we need to do is add a little something and everything will magically pop into place). The problem is far greater, for when people stop worshipping God they do not worship nothing; they worship anything. People are made to worship, to love, to put God first. And if they don't put him in that place they put something or someone else there, and that is the heart of sin.

False worship

Now I can understand you might be thinking at this point that I have moved a long way from being upset at my bike being vandalised to blaming the sin of the world on wrong worship. The point is that all sin, big and small, has its origin in getting worship wrong – so says Paul:

> The wrath of God is being revealed from heaven against all the godlessness and wickedness of men who suppress the

truth by their wickedness, since what may be known about God is plain to them, because God has made it plain to them. For since the creation of the world God's invisible qualities – his eternal power and divine nature – have been clearly seen, being understood from what has been made, so that men are without excuse. For although they knew God, they neither glorified him as God nor gave thanks to him, but their thinking became futile and their foolish hearts were darkened. Although they claimed to be wise, they became fools and exchanged the glory of the immortal God for images made to look like mortal man and birds and animals and reptiles. Therefore God gave them over in the sinful desires of their hearts to sexual impurity for the degrading of their bodies with one another. They exchanged the truth of God for a lie, and worshipped and served created things rather than the Creator – who is for ever praised. Amen. Because of this, God gave them over to shameful lusts. (Romans 1:18–26)

There are three stages at work here: God makes who he is plain to people; people choose to worship other things; God lets people have the consequences of their choices. God does not play hide and seek with his creation. He makes himself plain. He does not obscure himself and then get cross when we don't see him – like the child who finds the perfect hiding place and then can't understand why everybody else has given up on the game. God reveals who he is. He can't help it. And what is more, he has made a world that shouts out what kind of God he is.

From time to time I go to Switzerland as a seasonal chaplain with the Intercontinental Church Society. The ICS exists to tell English-speaking people about Jesus. There are permanent chaplains all over the globe sponsored by ICS, and also people like me who work as seasonal chaplains for a couple of weeks in the year at holiday spots across Europe. My favourite haunt is Wengen, high in the Swiss Alps, below the Eiger and Jungfrau mountains. It really is a spectacular place. The first time I went I was amazed as I stepped off the train to discover that Switzerland really was just how I'd imagined: I could hear cowbells! I could see snow-capped peaks. There were flower-covered meadows and chalets with roofs down to the ground. My hotel bedroom looked up to the Jungfrau, glorious in the afternoon sunlight, and in the valley below I could make out high waterfalls beginning to cascade to depths beyond my sight.

That first evening I sat out on the hotel veranda and chatted to one of the young holiday reps in the village. He said quite simply that a place like Wengen makes you stop and think about the deeper things in life.

A couple of days later I met a lovely couple from Yorkshire; farmers who were enjoying their first break for years. We were walking on the mountain top above the village. Gradually the conversation turned to Jesus, and they quite openly talked about faith and church and what they felt was true. Now, my experience of Yorkshire farmers is that they are not the most touchy-feely of people, but something about the grandeur and the majesty and the peace of the setting opened them up. It was a delight to welcome them into church on both of the Sundays I was there. Paul was right: creation spoke clearly to them of 'God's invisible qualities – his eternal power and divine nature'.

The sad thing is that most people refuse to see what is right in front of them. God does not hide himself, but like Adam and Eve in the Garden of Eden, we do. We avert our eyes from his gaze and go chasing after any other thing that glints in the light or takes our fancy. I made this point to a group of Christians once, a home group from my church, and one girl got a little cross with me. 'I've only been a Christian a year,' she said, 'and I don't agree with that point. I mean, a year ago I didn't think God made himself plain. I couldn't see him.'

So I said, 'OK, but you see him in the creation now?'

'Yes,' she replied.

'Is it the same creation?'

'Yes,' she replied.

'Is it the same God?'

'Yes.'

'Do you think God has been doing something different this last year to make himself clearer?'

She paused. 'I suppose that I'm the one who's changed. I can see him now, and maybe I could a bit before; but what about those who don't see?' Her fear was for her father, who was not a Christian.

So I said that clearly God was always around, always making himself known. If he'd opened her eyes to see what the apostle Paul says is there for us to see, perhaps she should carry on praying that he would do the same for her father. God makes clear who he is. The problem is, we choose to look away and follow and worship other gods, more attractive idols, easier objects of worship that cost less than the real thing.

What does it mean to worship idols? It means we put them first, we love them with all our heart and mind and soul. We think we are so wise, says Paul, yet we chase after the daftest things – things we make, things we desire, things we think will make us happy.

Sometimes we chase after good things, but the passion of the chase can turn good things bad. A mother should love her children, but when that love becomes obsession the children are going to be harmed. Worshipping her kids is going to turn them into little monsters, not little angels. And the very desire which is at the heart of the mother's obsession – that her children should have the very best – becomes impossible and self-defeating.

The world is full of people who worship the wrong things. And Paul has a special word for such people: he calls them 'fools'. They are fools because God makes himself plain and they choose other things, thinking their wisdom is greater than his, presuming that as members of creation their judgement is superior to the Creator's. And the result? You makes your choice and you takes your chance. All choices, big or small, have consequences.

'Marcus, would you like red or white wine?' Oh dear,

what a dilemma. I prefer red, but if the white is particularly nice, I'll miss out. I hate missing out. And if the red is good, I'll miss out more, because I enjoy that more. But I have to choose, and whatever I choose I have to live with.

Or as A-levels approach, you have to choose what universities to apply to, and then which one to go to. A life-changing choice. Most people get to make it only once, and that choice will choose friends, career, place to live, even perhaps a partner – everything for years to come. If you choose Oxford, you will never meet those people from London. They will never be your friends. You will never do that course in Edinburgh. That career will not happen.

Choosing to worship God, to put him first, to love him with all we have and are, means that we choose to put the world the right way up. We choose the right relationship with the Maker of all things. We choose life in all its fullness. When we choose to worship the world, or anything in it, rather than the Creator, we choose to worship the transient – things that will decay – and our lives reflect the choice we make. God will allow us the appropriate result of our worship choice. As Louie Giglio puts it, 'We become what we worship. If you don't like who you're becoming, take a quick inventory of the things on the throne of your heart.'[1]

Sin is not just offending the moral sensibilities of

1. Louie Giglio, *The Air I Breathe* (Multnomah Publishers, 2003),
   p. 35.

some great 'spy in the sky'. It is fracturing the intended
creation order – the way things are meant to be. 'Man,
made more like God than any other creature, has
become less like God than any other creature. Created
to reflect the glory of God, he has retreated sullenly into
his cave – reflecting only his own sinfulness.'[2] Failing to
worship our Maker leads down a one-way street to the
collapse of human society. It is the ultimate sin, and for
it, as a world, we are paying the ultimate price.

The common condition

Getting worship wrong, or worshipping the wrong things
to put it the other way round, is the common condition
of humanity in a fallen world. We are all sucked into the
process, and there seems to be no way out. Even the best
of people make the same old mistakes.

Solomon was given the task of building the first
temple for God in Jerusalem. As the temple was
finished, the priests and everybody celebrated, and the
power of God came in a remarkable way. Solomon
prayed God's blessing on the work of the temple, and
again the glory of the Lord filled the place. It was a red-
letter day in the history of God's people. But that night
the Lord appeared to Solomon and spoke to him. Let's
look at what God said, and remember the occasion of
his speaking.

---

2. A.W. Tozer, *Whatever Happened to Worship?* (Kingsway
   Publications, 1986), p. 52.

If my people, who are called by my name, will humble
themselves and pray and seek my face and turn from their
wicked ways, then will I hear from heaven and will forgive
their sin and will heal their land. Now my eyes will be open
and my ears attentive to the prayers offered in this place. I
have chosen and consecrated this temple so that my Name
may be there for ever. My eyes and my heart will always be
there.

As for you, if you walk before me as David your father
did, and do all I command, and observe my decrees and
laws, I will establish your royal throne, as I covenanted with
David your father when I said, 'You shall never fail to have
a man to rule over Israel.'

But if you turn away and forsake the decrees and
commands I have given you and go off to serve other gods
and worship them, then I will uproot Israel from my land,
which I have given them, and will reject this temple which
I have consecrated for my Name. I will make it a byword
and an object of ridicule among all peoples. And though
this temple is now so imposing, all who pass by will be
appalled and say, 'Why has the Lord done such a thing to
this land and to this temple?' People will answer, 'Because
they have forsaken the Lord, the God of their fathers, who
brought them out of Egypt, and have embraced other
gods, worshipping and serving them – that is why he
brought all this disaster on them.' (2 Chronicles 7:14–22)

Sin is worshipping anybody or anything that is not God,
and it carries consequences. But you would think that if
anybody could get this right it would be Solomon, who
built the temple and had such massive experiences of
the Lord, and such warnings from him. Yet in 1 Kings 11

we see that Solomon married many foreign women, about whom the Lord had commanded, 'You must not intermarry with them, because they will surely turn your hearts after their gods.' Solomon married 700 of them, and kept a further 300 as concubines. And they did turn his heart away from God as he grew older, and he built shrines for these foreign gods, these idols, in Jerusalem. So God allowed Solomon the consequences of his choices, and what follows in the books of Kings is a tale of woe after woe as king after king worships false gods and idols.

Ahab is described as the worst of the lot in 1 Kings 21:25: 'He behaved in the vilest manner by going after idols.' He is not accused of any great moral lapse, of eating babies or murdering his grandmother. He is the worst of the lot because his idolatry, his wrong worship, is the worst. Contrast that with David, the great king, the king after God's own heart (1 Samuel 13:14). Did he never sin? He is certainly presented as the ideal king. Yet straight away our minds are filled with the story of his adultery with Bathsheba, and his subsequent murder of Uriah her husband. Why does this not disqualify David in the way that Ahab's acts disqualified him from receiving God's blessing? Why does this sin not seem to count as much? Because it was an aberration. It was a serious sin, and David paid seriously for it, but it was not the fruit of a wicked life. It was an exception in a good life. In what way a good life? A life of worship. Ahab's sins were worship sins – sins that betrayed a whole life lived away from God. Even in the immediate aftermath of

David's sin, as he waited and the son born of adultery died, he displayed the heart that God loved. When he heard the news about the baby's death, 'He went into the house of the Lord and worshipped' (2 Samuel 12:20).

But David was an exception among the kings. Most were more like Ahab, worshipping idols. We know little of their moral fibre, whether or not they were what our society would think of as 'good men'. They are condemned by the Bible writers for the kind of sin our society does not begin to take seriously: the sin of not worshipping the Lord God. Our values are not the Bible's. But even God's leaders forgot what was most important. Occasionally, true enough, in the story of the kings some good man comes along and tries to stop the rot. But Israel, the people of God, led by her anointed kings, will have none of it, and the trend becomes irreversible – to the point where just after 600 BC, God allows the Babylonians to sack Jerusalem and destroy the temple. The destruction God warned Solomon about has come to pass.

But that should not surprise us: sadden us, yes – surprise us, no. Go back to that picture of Solomon in the temple. The man who knew best the blessing of God and the power of his presence in worship, and who knew the warning of God – that all he had gained would become a wasteland and desolate if he worshipped false gods – this man got worship wrong. What hope does anybody else have of doing better?

Sin destroyed the people of God. It destroyed their

city, their country and their temple as the Lord allowed them the appropriate result of their worship choices. And the nature of the sin that did this great evil was the root nature of all sin: getting worship wrong. Jeremiah expresses the heart of God, 'Why have they provoked me to anger with their images, with their worthless foreign idols?' (Jeremiah 8:19).

Our experience

Solomon's condition is ours. We know that to worship God is best, and we must love him with all we have and are; put him first. But somehow we still chase after other things. True, few of them actually claim a religious significance, but they take our hearts captive and turn us to loving and serving things that are not God as surely as if they were idols in shrines.

Once and only once have I played the National Lottery. I don't know what your opinion of that is. I know what it did to me. It was early on in its history. I was in my first curacy in South Wales, and I decided to buy a ticket mainly because my boss was so violently against the whole thing. The rebel in me wanted something to do. So I handed over my money and waited for the evening's show on TV. And as I waited, I spent the day discovering what covetousness really is. I coveted a new car, a new stereo, a new everything. To be sure, I mentally tithed all I was about to receive, then I put that out of my mind and enjoyed spending time thinking of spending all that money.

Of course I won nothing. But I gained a valuable insight into the way people's minds work. For a day I worshipped money. I don't normally, but that day I did. It came first, it controlled my thinking, it took all my mind and soul and strength. And that, my friend, is sin. Anything that takes that place in life is taking God's place. It is wrong worship. You may not go to a money temple and sing songs to money about the goodness of money, but it is worship none the less.

Don't waste your worship on some little god, squandering your birthright on idols made only with human imagination. Guard your worship . . . and carefully evaluate all potential takers. To choose well doesn't mean we can't appreciate things of beauty and style. It's certainly not wrong to deeply love another. Nor is it a sin to value a great job or enjoy an amazing destination. But when we elevate any of these things to the highest place in our hearts, we've gone too far.[3]

Stop for a moment and think about this. You may not sing songs to your job, or listen to sermon tapes about your ideal life partner or pray to the bank manager or set up a shrine to the TV or bow before the garden centre or consciously think of the car manual as Scripture, but if any of these things (or anything else) assumes first place in life – the place where everything revolves around them, where they take your energy and

3. Louie Giglio, *The Air I Breathe,* p. 29.

concentration and where you need them to live – then you are worshipping something that is not God.

It is the common condition, it is our experience. Everybody worships. It is as simple as that. But in a fallen, sinful world, everybody worships the wrong thing. Adam and Eve began it. Indeed they typify the whole idea. The serpent tempted Eve into eating what she knew she shouldn't by saying that then she would 'be like God' (Genesis 3:5). It was not enough to be made 'in the image of God' (Genesis 1:27). Not enough to reflect his glory. Not enough to have the highest position in the created order. They wanted to be the same as God, to be worthy of worship themselves, to be as good as him, to be the focus of self-worship. This was the first sin. And it is still the most popular.

The repair shop

So I am left on the wrong side of town, with a broken bike and a bad temper. Because people get worship wrong, the whole world is in a mess. Is that all there is? Am I stuck out here because humanity is stuck in this endlessly repeating cycle of wrong worship that leads to all sorts of sin that leads to wrong worship? It's not just my bike I want fixed; it's all creation! I don't want the symptoms cured; I want the disease that is killing us all sorted once and for all. Is there a repair shop for the souls of humanity? Can anybody help?

2

Perfect Worship - the Cross

If I ask someone a question, normally I expect a reply in terms set by the question. What I mean is, if I ask, 'What is two plus two?' I don't expect the answer 'Red shirts'. 'Red shirts' might have been a great answer had the question been 'What do two United players and two Liverpool players have in common?' But that was not the question I asked, so it is a useless answer. I was looking for an answer more along the lines of 'Four'.

It's a bit like Jim Bowen on *Bull's-eye*, which, for the uninitiated, was a TV quiz show based on playing darts that Jim used to present. One member of a two-player team had to throw a dart and then the other would have to answer a question correctly in order to continue. It was never a favourite show of mine but Jim Bowen had one stock phrase I will never forget. If a contestant got a question wrong, he could not bear to tell them. It would go something like this: Jim would say, 'Where are the Houses of Parliament?' And the contestant would look very scared and eventually say something like, 'Er, is it Denmark, Jim?' And Jim, bless him, would reply in the phrase I loved, 'That's a good answer, but it's not what I'm looking for.' 'No, Jim, it was not a good answer,' I used to scream at the TV. 'It's wrong!' Of course he had a point. If the question had been different, it may well have been an excellent answer! If he had asked where Danish people come from, then the dart-throwing team-mate would have been all lined up for the next stage in the game. But Denmark, in the terms the question set, was not a good answer; it was a wrong answer. No points, no prizes.

If sin is the great problem with the world, and if sin is fundamentally about wrong worship, then the answer to the problem must also fundamentally be about worship. But to be the right solution it must be about right worship. If not, however good an answer it is, it is not the answer to our problem.

Now, being the good Christian you are, you know full well that the answer to sin is Jesus' death on the cross, and that does not seem to be about worship, does it? Except that we are trying to see what worship has to do with the big issues of our faith, and that means we are not simply doing a word-search on 'worship' through the Bible. It's the ideas that count, not just the words.

For instance, I could talk to people from a certain church – let's call it St Barnabas – and say, 'That was great. The band were on good form, we sang for 40 minutes and God really showed up.' And these people would have clearly heard me say, 'We worshipped God,' though I'd not used those words. The idea was there. The words I used painted a picture. To people from another church – let's call it St Mary's – I might have said, 'That was glorious. The whole place was candlelit, the choir was superb and there was a real sense of eternal things.' These people too just heard me say, 'We worshipped God.' They didn't hear it when I talked about the worship experience at St Barnabas, as it was not their context. But now they are happy – though the folk from St B's think I've just been to a concert. What you are used to, the words you use to describe worship, may be different from what others are used to – though the experience of God and worshipping him, the idea behind the words, may be equally valid across a range of styles of Christian service.

My point is this: the Bible, I believe, clearly describes Jesus' death on the cross in terms of the perfect act of worship. But its terms of reference are not ones we are used to, as we have no direct contact with Judaism based around the temple at the time of Jesus. We are like the folk from St Barnabas hearing the guys from St Mary's talk about worship. It's just not where we are at. So before I can show how the Bible sees the cross of Christ as worship, and worship that is so perfect it reverses for good all the effects of humanity's wrong worship, first we must look at the way the Jews worshipped at the temple.

The Bible actually gives two answers to the problem of sin. The first is the temple sacrifice system of the Old

Testament. It has the merit for us of clearly being about worship, but the drawback of not exactly working. The second, the cross, we may not often think of as being worship, but it has the merit of working well. We need to take a look at both together.

The worship that failed

We saw in Chapter 1 that the Old Testament Law begins with commands about worship. Begins, and continues for some time. The whole idea of Israel as the people of God was that they should be a worshipping people, living under the Law that taught them how to be God's people, loving him and each other, so that the nations of the world would see them and say, 'Oh, I see. So God is like that.' Of course, the first problem here is that Israel too existed in a world full of sin. So a system of sacrifices was commanded in the Law in order to keep the people right with God. They would get things wrong, then make sacrifices to get right with God again. James Dunn says:

> Judaism was a religion of forgiveness. The whole cult was geared to the restoration and maintenance of a positive relation between God and his people. The sacrificial system, particularly the sin offering and the day of atonement, was designed precisely to provide forgiveness.[1]

---

1. James Dunn, *The Parting of the Ways* (SCM, 1991), p. 45.

The worship set up in the Law by God for his people was all about forgiving his people, and the way it was to be done was through ceremonies that were based around sacrifices. And that might mean killing a bird or a goat or a bull, or it might mean offering grain or waving sheaves of corn around. Leviticus 23 takes us through the major festivals of the Jewish year – though these just provided a focus for temple worship. Sacrifices were going on the whole time. And if you were a Jew living at the time of the temple, when you heard the word 'sacrifice', you heard the word 'worship'.

The reason these sacrifices were offered as an answer to the problem of sin is that they marked the reversal of the trend to wrong worship we talked about in Chapter 1. You took a part of creation and offered it back to God, who made it. Instead of Adam's sin of looking to the creation rather than the Creator, you placed a token of all that God had made in your hands and offered it back to him. You looked up, not down; you worshipped God. It is the opposite of what we saw Paul describe in Romans 1.

But there was more than this. Israel was God's chosen people. In worship, as they sacrificed to him, they met at his appointed place – at the tabernacle in Moses' day and at the temple after Solomon. The life the priests sacrificed in that place was a sign that all their lives were sacrificed to God, and that action in that place strangely assured them of forgiveness. In the Jewish year there were particular moments when these

ideas came to the fore: the Feast of Passover marked
how God chose and delivered his people when they
were slaves in Egypt; the Day of Atonement took everyone to the mercy seat in the temple, and the sacrifice
made there demonstrated how God in his grace forgave
their sins. As the Jews worshipped God, they saw that
the helpless were helped, the sinful were forgiven.
Surely this was the answer to the problem of wrong
worship?

Yes and no. It is a question of symptoms and causes.
Have you ever flown on a plane when you have had a
cold? It is not recommended. The pressure that builds
on your sinuses is remarkable. A couple of times I have
had to do this, and the best thing to help I have found
are those little Karvol capsules – the ones that you break
on to tissues and breathe in. Boy, if that doesn't clear
your passages, nothing will. It cures the symptoms, at
least enough for you to get by. But it does not deal with
the cold that lies at the root of your problem.

The sacrifices of the Old Covenant, the sacrifices
described in the Law, are just like those Karvol capsules.
They deal with the symptoms but leave the disease
undealt with. See what the writer to the Hebrews says in
the New Testament:

The law is only a shadow of the good things that are
coming – not the realities themselves. For this reason it can
never, by the same sacrifices repeated endlessly year after
year, make perfect those who draw near to worship. If it
could, would they not have stopped being offered? For the

worshippers would have been cleansed once for all, and would no longer have felt guilty for their sins. But those sacrifices are an annual reminder of sins, because it is impossible for the blood of bulls and goats to take away sins. (Hebrews 10:1–4)

The problem is simple: the sin of wrong worship. Putting anything else in the place of God and letting it have what should be God's alone – this sin is at the heart of the human condition. The Old Testament Law shows that something needs to be done, indeed can be done. But all it actually manages to do is deal with the outward signs of sin, for if it really worked, why would people need to keep going back and making new sacrifices, killing new animals, offering new grain and birds and promises? Bulls and goats can't cut the mustard. Outwardly you walk away sorted, feeling good about God and about yourself. But inside nothing has changed. And that means that although hands and eyes have looked up from the creation to the Creator as they worshipped, hearts were unchanged. And people who have chosen to worship the creation rather than the Creator have engaged in an act that ultimately has made no difference. Forgiveness has been offered, but remains a stranger. Sure, we have some kind of answer, and it comes in the right sort of terms, but the problem is bigger – too big for this answer.

The worship that works

Where to start? Let's go back to Romans. After all, it was Paul who started us down this path by pointing out that the problem with the world is wrong worship. If that is the problem, what is his solution?

> But now a righteousness from God, apart from law, has been made known, to which the Law and the Prophets testify. This righteousness from God comes through faith in Jesus Christ to all who believe. There is no difference, for all have sinned and fall short of the glory of God, and are justified freely by his grace through the redemption that came by Christ Jesus. God presented him as a sacrifice of atonement, through faith in his blood. (Romans 3:21–25)

The Old Testament Law didn't work, says Paul; people just couldn't keep it. It told us what to do, but we didn't do it. So now God has put us right with him a different way – although in fact the Old Testament scriptures prepared us for it, both by prophesying what God would do, and by giving us a context, a worldview, that would help us understand. And that worldview has everything to do with temple worship.

This is the crux of Paul's argument, the answer to the problems of the world he has described, and it comes in worship language. First he talks of the 'redemption that came by Christ Jesus'. Now I should say that scholars argue over the precise meanings of these words, but for the average Jewish Christian hearing Paul's words for the first time, 'redemption' is essentially a picture of the Passover and Exodus, where God brought his people out of slavery in Egypt and delivered them to freedom in the Promised Land. Every Passover festival, this picture of redemption was major in the Jewish mind. It was the key worship image. Indeed, at the start of Romans 6, Paul returns to talking about the cross. Here he talks of being baptised into Christ's death and raised to a new life: for a Jew an essential part of this imagery has to do with the journey through the Red Sea during the Exodus, when the people left Egypt. Going through the Red Sea was like baptism – the people died to their old life in Egypt as we have the idea in Christian baptism of dying to sin. That life had gone. Crossing the Red Sea was the point of no return. Arriving on the other side and then the eventual arrival in the Promised Land was like being born to a new life. Paul himself describes that journey as being 'baptised into Moses' (1 Corinthians 10:2). Redemption is worship language. God helps the helpless. He buys a people sold into slavery – slavery to sin, to wrong worship. He's buying them back so they can worship in truth.

But Passover is not the only worship festival on display in Romans 3. 'God presented him as a sacrifice of atonement' takes us to the Day of Atonement, where the sin of the whole people was dealt with, year after year. Except that at the end of the day, that sacrifice of worship did not achieve its aim. It merely showed the way to the one sacrifice that would come and really deal with sin, with the problem of wrong worship, looking to the creation instead of the Creator. Jesus is the perfect sacrifice of atonement, the perfect worship offering.

Why? Again we have to stay in the Jewish worship picture. On the Day of Atonement, the priest making the sacrifice first had to sacrifice an offering for his own sin. The whole process acknowledges the impossibility of what is going on. Even the guy doing the sacrificing is as guilty as everyone else. But now God presents Jesus as the offering. God takes the role of the priest, the one leading the people in worship. God leads the worship and things are looking up. What was the animal doing in the sacrifice? It was a representative. It was representing the people; it had the people's sin symbolically placed on it, though it was an innocent victim. 'From his cross rings salvation's song, declaring to all that redemption has come . . . The cross of Christ is a place of peace. And the place where true worship begins.'[2]

Jesus is no innocent victim, for although he is without sin and his whole life has been pure worship of the Father, he is also Messiah, the chosen one, the true and proper representative of the people of God. This is not a barbaric human sacrifice to appease an angry God. This is God in Jesus being and doing what he called his whole people to be and do: to love God with all your heart and all your soul and all your strength. Jesus is being an obedient worshipper obediently worshipping. It may not look like worship to the crowd from St

2. Louie Giglio, *The Air I Breathe* (Multnomah Publishers, 2003), p. 45.

Barnabas I described earlier – there is no band, no 40 minutes of singing. The folk from St Mary's are equally confused: where are the candles and the choir? But it is worship. Israel failed to worship God worthily, consistently, even though they were his chosen people. But Jesus succeeds. He is the true Israel, the servant who is always obedient – obedient even to death.

More than this. The Old Testament worship of the temple needed things to be done in the right place. Where is all this being done in Romans 3? The word translated as 'sacrifice of atonement' in Greek is *hilasterion*, which is the word in the Greek version of the Old Testament that Paul himself would have used for the mercy seat, the place where the sacrifice had to be made: the place in the temple where God showed mercy and forgave the people. Paul uses a word which not only captures the meaning of the sacrifice, the means of worship, but also the very place of worship. Jesus offers the perfect worship in the perfect place.

Let's recap. The cross is where God redeems his people, which speaks of the Passover festival, the ending of slavery to sin and the beginning of a new life of freedom to worship anew. Jesus on the cross is the sacrifice of atonement through which God forgives the people's sin, forgives the wrong worship that has filled our lives. The cross is the place of forgiveness, the mercy seat where Israel celebrated the Day of Atonement.

Imagine a huge conference, filled with Christians coming to worship, a sort of mega-Spring Harvest/New Wine/Soul Survivor all rolled into one and increased

dramatically in size. Hundreds of thousands of worshippers gathering together. That's the Passover festival.
That's when Jesus died.

Do you see that for Paul the question of sin is a question of worship warped, and the solution of the cross is
the answer of worship won back to God, perfectly, by
the Son of God giving himself for his people? All the
language used is worship language. This *is* the answer
to our problem. It *does* fit. We don't need Jim Bowen's
platitude from *Bull's-eye*, because this answer is right. It
works. It comes in the same terms as the question.

Run that by me again . . .

What are we doing here? We are looking at the big
picture. We believe that big picture is all about us
worshipping God. That's the point of everything. Now if
that is true, then the Bible has to be full of this stuff; full
of the idea of people worshipping God being the big
picture. And if that is so, then we need to look beyond
Paul and his mates singing in jail at midnight, or even
beyond Solomon and his mates having a major Holy
Spirit session in the temple. We need to see if the big
ideas in the Bible have anything to do with worship.
Because if they do not, then how can worshipping God
be the big picture?

It's like being a Manchester United fan. (Or Leeds or
Liverpool, just come with me and don't worry too much
if United aren't your team. Somebody will be praying
for you.) If you came to my house, convinced I was a

United fan, you would expect to find signs of it all around. You might look for posters on the wall, perhaps a calendar too. You'd open the wardrobe and expect to find at least one shirt, and maybe other stuff like a fleece with a crest on it, or a club tie. Oh look, there are the videos – there must be at least the Treble video there, for surely every United supporter on the planet has that. Not to mention books and scarves and programmes and match tickets. But if you came and found nothing – no posters or videos or shirts or anything – then you might begin to have doubts. You might begin to feel I wasn't the real thing. You might begin to doubt that United played any part of real significance in my life at all.[3]

So we need to look at the big ideas in the Bible. We need to look at sin and the cross and salvation to see if the marks of worship are here. Because if they are not, then worshipping God cannot be the big picture. The big ideas make up the big picture. The premiss of this book only works if they all work together. And they do. Let's go back to the book of Hebrews.

True worship in Hebrews

We have already seen the critique of the Old Covenant made by the writer to the Hebrews earlier in this chapter. Essentially it's a grand idea, but it just doesn't work.

---

3. For the record, I do not currently own a club tie. I must do something about that.

So what does work?

> When Christ came as high priest of the good things that
> are already here, he went through the greater and more
> perfect tabernacle that is not man-made, that is to say, not
> a part of this creation. He did not enter by means of the
> blood of goats and calves; but he entered the Most Holy
> Place once for all by his own blood, having obtained eter-
> nal redemption. The blood of goats and bulls and the ashes
> of a heifer sprinkled on those who are ceremonially unclean
> sanctify them so that they are outwardly clean. How much
> more, then, will the blood of Christ, who through the eter-
> nal Spirit offered himself unblemished to God, cleanse our
> consciences from acts that lead to death, so that we may
> serve the living God! (Hebrews 9:11–14)

Are the people from St Barnabas starting to hear the
choir? Are the folk of St Mary's liking the guitars yet?
Are we getting used to the different worship context in
which these New Testament guys wrote?

Two things are happening in this passage from
Hebrews, and they are inextricably linked together. First,
we are having Christ's death on the cross described and
explained to us; and second, we are having that done
entirely in worship language. As in Romans 3 the twin
ideas of redemption (Passover) and forgiveness (Day of
Atonement) are paramount. As in Romans 3 the context
is the temple sacrifices. As in Romans 3 Jesus is
described as the perfect sacrifice. The old system deals
with the symptoms, but now Jesus has got to the heart
of the matter; he has cured the disease! No more need

for those Karvol capsules. He's got rid of the entire cold!

The redemption the Law provided was a matter of an historical event and a yearly remembering. But the redemption Jesus provides is eternal. It lasts for ever. It does not fade with memory or live on only in repeated ritual. It is the real thing. Real worship has won real results.

The forgiveness of the Law was a symbolic thing, a matter of ceremonies that demonstrated how necessary forgiveness was without ever truly making it happen. But the blood shed by Jesus' sacrifice cleanses the conscience. True worship truly cleanses.

So the verdict is made clear by the results: is this real, true, perfect worship? Well, look at what it does to us! This worship sacrifice of Jesus is the answer to the problem of sin, because it really works; it really makes a difference. Here are a few more verses from this section of Hebrews:

Day after day every priest stands and performs his religious duties; again and again he offers the same sacrifices, which can never take away sins. But when this priest [Jesus] had offered for all time one sacrifice for sins, he sat down at the right hand of God. Since that time he waits for his enemies to be made his footstool, because by one sacrifice he has made perfect for ever those who are being made holy.

The Holy Spirit also testifies to us about this. First he says: 'This is the covenant I will make with them after that time, says the Lord. I will put my laws in their hearts, and I will write them on their minds.' Then he adds: 'Their sins and lawless acts I will remember no more.' And where these have been forgiven, there is no longer any sacrifice for sin. (Hebrews 10:11–18)

It is worship that got us into this mess (wrong worship, focusing on the wrong things – on creation, things made, not the Maker) and it was worship that God gave to Israel to get them out of the mess. Only it didn't work. The problem was too big, the people too sinful. So then God sent his Son, his only Son, whose love and worship of the Father was so perfect that he gave himself as a sacrifice for sin. And this act of worship worked. This one made all the others irrelevant. This one actually did away with all the wrong worship the world had ever known. The temple worship of the Jews made a person ceremonially clean; that is to say, they were sorted, but only on the outside; this worship worked skin deep. But now, the worship of Jesus on the cross reaches hearts and minds, and transforms from within. It really works. It really makes a difference. It really brings forgiveness, not just a show.

When I started to look at Hebrews, I did so because many books on worship quote verses from there, so I felt I needed to know more. After a while, I felt that I could not use any of this material, because worship was only the metaphor, not the subject of Hebrews. Clearly the writer is talking about the differences between the Old and New Covenants, the way God dealt with people in the Old Testament, and the way he deals with us now, post-Jesus. Worship is just the language he uses to point out the differences. But then I began to ask,

'Why choose worship language? Why put simple ideas in such a complex way?'

Then I began to see it: worship is more than the metaphor. Sure, the difference between the covenants is the core of the book, but perhaps worship is the core of the covenants too. For if worship is the big picture, if the Bible is all about the way to worship God in spirit and in truth, then how else do you describe what was going on on the cross except in these terms?

David Peterson in *Engaging With God* puts these ideas very helpfully together:

> Christ's blood breaks the old oscillating pattern of defilement and cleansing. The ongoing problem of sin made it necessary for rites of cleansing and re-consecration to be repeated under the old covenant year after year (cf.10:4). The blood of Jesus, however, provides a once-for-all cleansing and consecration to the service of God under the new covenant (cf. 9:14, 13:12). Thus the sacrifice of Christ is foundational to a Christian theology of worship.[4]

Without the cross of Christ, the best we can hope for is a swinging between extremes: now we worship the world, now we worship God. This is because nothing changes our hearts, so even if we try our hardest, we will always muck up at some point. We will never be consistently good enough. Sure, worship will be constant, but its object will vary; that is, we will always

---

4. David Peterson, *Engaging with God* (Apollos, 1992) p. 237.

worship something, but the chances are it will not be God. But Jesus redraws this map of failure by his completely successful worship of the Father. And therefore, in Peterson's words, 'the sacrifice of Christ is foundational to a Christian theology of worship'. What Jesus did alters what we can do.

And that is the gospel. That's the good news. That's why Jesus' death is so exciting for us. It is not just a doctrine thing; it changes the whole world for us. We are used to the idea of sin messing up the world and Jesus sorting it out, but now we see these are worship issues. Wrong worship messes up the world, but perfect worship sorts it out. The question for us is how we can join in this perfect worship. How can we become part of the solution instead of being the problem?

But I'm running ahead of myself. We've spent some time gazing at the cross of Christ, but now there is an empty tomb before us. The stone is rolled away, and before we can begin to understand what this means for us, we are confronted with a risen Lord. The resurrection of Jesus demonstrates the true power of what he has done. So having stood with the first disciples at the foot of the cross, now let's spend some time with our exalted Lord Jesus.

3

Jesus Is Lord: So What?

'Jesus is Lord, creation's voice proclaims it'; 'He is Lord, he is Lord, he is risen from the dead and he is Lord'; 'He is the Lord and he reigns on high'; 'Lord, I lift your name on high'. These are all song titles. You probably recognise them. Songs that are sung in all sorts of churches up and down the land. Songs which celebrate the fact that since the resurrection, Christian communities have always seen Jesus as Lord over all things – even life and death. But what do these words mean? Actually, what does this one word, 'Lord', mean?

I once led a school assembly in the song 'Blessed is the King who comes'. It's a good rousing song, with lots of actions and stomping about. The second verse says 'Majestic is the King', and I felt that I wanted to be sure the children knew what the word 'majestic' meant. After all, it's pointless them singing something that is meaningless – like listening to pop songs on the radio and singing gobbledegook because you never could quite make out what they were saying in verse two. Anyway, a very serious looking little girl aged about seven put her hand up quickly and confidently, so I said, 'Go on then – what does majestic mean?'

Without any hesitation or fear of being wrong, she looked me in the eye and replied, 'The Easter Bunny.' Now, in his own special way the Easter Bunny may well be majestic, but I'm quite sure that's not most people's understanding of the word! And I am equally sure that most people in churches today happily sing about Jesus being Lord without giving a second thought to what they are singing. After all, it's just a word, isn't it?

Well, yes, it is just a word. But words have meanings. That's how we communicate. I say the word 'Cow', and you think of a big animal that gives milk or beef or financial headaches to farmers. These are some of the meanings attributed to the word. But in worship, sometimes words become so familiar that the meanings disappear.

For example, I remember when I first learned the song 'By your side I would stay'. To me it was just another song, but a friend of mine, Ruth, was amazed at the intimacy of that picture of being with Jesus. She heard the words, heard what they said and what they meant, and the power of that image of familiarity was so strong that at first she could hardly bear to sing it.

The word 'Lord' is, I think, of all our worship words perhaps one of the least understood. But it is one of the most biblical words we use, as well as one of the most frequent. When Jesus was raised from the dead, the word 'Lord' gained new importance. In Luke's Gospel, the phrase 'the Lord Jesus' first appears at the start of chapter 24, the resurrection chapter. In Philippians 2, God gives Jesus the title 'Lord' because he was obedient to death. In John 20, Thomas loses all his doubts as he cries out, 'My Lord and my God!'

Power talk

One of the reasons we do not dwell on the word 'Lord' is because for our culture it is a power word. 'Jesus is Lord' is a power statement, and we get very nervous about this sort of thing. We expect people to abuse power, because it gets abused everywhere we turn: at home, at work, even at church. We especially shy away from absolute power, which (we presume) corrupts absolutely. After all, our role models for absolute power – that is, total control – are a pretty mean bunch: Adolf Hitler, Joseph Stalin, Saddam Hussein. These are hardly positive role models.

So, instead, when we hear the word 'Lord', we engage in a little theological revisionism. In other words, we change the meaning to suit us. We are afraid of power claims that might be too great, and 'Lord' sounds quite big, so we redefine it in culturally more acceptable terms. Some people say 'Jesus is Lord' but mean 'Jesus is like a president'. Others say the same words but mean 'Jesus is prime minister' or 'Jesus is a constitutional monarch like the Queen'. We do not know what Lord means, so we instead think in terms we do understand. It's about power, and who has power over us? The government. So Jesus must be like them. The problem is not just our making God like any one person or group of people; it is that all our understanding of political power – and even power within many churches – is based on democracy. We vote. We choose. We elect. We decide. And we can change our minds.

Democracy is a poor model for understanding God. Listen to these words as God speaks to Job:

> Where were you when I laid the earth's foundation? Tell me, if you understand. Who marked off its dimensions? Surely you know! Who stretched a measuring line across it? On what were its footings set, or who laid its cornerstone – while the morning stars sang together and all the angels shouted for joy? (Job 38:4–7)

> Can you pull in the leviathan with a fishhook or tie down his tongue with a rope? Can you put a cord through his nose or pierce his jaw with a hook? Will he keep begging you for mercy? Will he speak to you with gentle words? Will he make an agreement with you for you to take him as your slave for life? Can you make a pet of him like a bird or put him on a leash for your girls? (Job 41:1–5)

God speaks poetically of the enormity of his power and then asks Job whether he thinks he is equal to it. And of course he isn't, for God's power is greater than any person's: greater than any president's or prime minister's or king's. All our earthly power analogies are flawed, yet because they are the ways our culture experiences power, they are images that have influence on our thinking about and understanding of Jesus. To understand what the Bible has to say about the lordship of Christ, how God's power is his power, and how that affects our worship, we again have to understand the culture of those who wrote the Scriptures. What did this word 'Lord' mean to the people who wrote it? It meant worship. To hear the word 'Lord' was to worship. To hear 'Lord Jesus' was to fall and adore him. We sing the word and feel nothing. This is not biblical behaviour. So why did the early church respond as they did? What was different for them?

If we want to regain the Bible's power to worship the Lord Jesus, we need to look at the meeting of two worldviews, two contexts, two ways of living – a meeting place where the early Christians lived and worked every day of their lives. We need to look at it and learn for ourselves what came naturally to them. For the church was born into a world governed by the might of Rome but interpreted by the Scriptures of Israel. And both had quite a lot to say on the subject of lordship.

When in Rome . . .

The Roman Empire was ruled by Caesar. As an absolute monarch, Caesar took the biscuit! And in addition to the economic, social and legal spheres of life, he had power over the religious too, with both the imperial cult (the worship of the emperor) and the whole Roman range of gods from Apollo to Venus existing to promote Roman imperial values. Absolute power in every sphere, and not in a nice middle-class way, but at times making our Hitlers and Stalins look rather weak-kneed.

Now it must be noted that the word 'Lord' in its Latin form of *dominus* or the Greek *kyrios*, is not by itself a claim to being God; it is simply a power word. The extent of the power claimed has to be explained by other words. It's the same in English: Lord Archer doesn't claim to be God by using the title 'lord'. When in court, the participants in a legal case do not think they are in the presence of a minor deity every time they say 'my lord' to the judge. It takes a little more than that to get the word to mean God.

The emperors found that little extra. Nero declared himself 'Lord of all creation'. Domitian expected to be referred to as 'Lord and God'. The Christian martyrs who refused to acknowledge Caesar as lord were not making the political point of certain Jewish radicals in those days (the Sycarii, who refused the political power of the Roman state), but a religious point that the state had no religious power because that belonged to God, and Jesus to whom he had given it. The reason emperors wanted religious power was quite simply because it was the ultimate power – if you had that, you had all power, and everyone would have to obey you. The vast array of Roman gods was made to boost the imperial authority, but when the emperors started to claim direct religious power, even these gods became unnecessary. Quite simply, you had to obey the emperor's whim on any given subject at any given time. Through the might of his armies, he enforced absolute obedience on every issue, from the cradle to the grave, and (as he claimed the status of a god) ultimately beyond the grave too.

It was this ultimate claim that Christians opposed. They contrasted Nero's title of 'The lord our Emperor' with their own description of Jesus as 'My Lord, the King of kings and Emperor of all peoples'. They understood the extent of the power claim made by the emperors and they understood that while it was wrong in imperial hands it was right in Jesus' hands. That understanding led many to take up the martyr's mantle. There was only one who could claim such obedience. So although it was true, and on one level a simple confession of faith, given the stakes no wonder Paul commented that 'no-one can say, "Jesus is Lord," except by the Holy Spirit' (1 Corinthians 12:3).

It was not the nature of the power that was wrong; it was the one who was claiming it. I recently met Simon, a school friend I had not seen for ten years. He told me of another chap we had known at school, Ian, whose main memory of me was that I once locked a teacher out of our classroom. I have to say that I do not remember doing this, but it is (sadly!) very believable. I could have done it. Now in a school, it is not wrong for somebody to be kept outside a classroom – that power of exclusion is quite acceptable. But only when a teacher is keeping a child out. It is quite unacceptable the other way round. If I ever did that, I was way out of line. Not because the power was wrong, but because I was the

wrong person to wield it. So the early church understood absolute power over all things and the emperor.
Absolute power over all things, including the spiritual
life, is right and proper. But not in the emperor's hands.

Put bluntly, the Roman version of lordship was blasphemy, but the blasphemy was not that it claimed
ridiculous power, the sort of thing no one should have;
rather the blasphemy was that a man, the emperor,
claimed the extent of power that only belongs to God.
In our culture, our world, we look at things differently,
and looking at this claim we make a different assump-
tion: we see it as ridiculous power that God should want
to rule our thinking, our doing, our speaking, our being.
He can have influence, sure, but I'm in charge of me.
This is quite a change in outlook.

Let's have a look at a biblical example. John in the
book of Revelation does not see this absolute power as
ridiculous power, though in the wrong hands clearly it is
unthinkable: 'Men worshipped the dragon because he
had given authority to the beast, and they also
worshipped the beast and asked, "Who is like the beast?
Who can make war against him?"' (Revelation 13:4).
The beast is the empire. Look at the song the people
sang about the beast, and contrast it with Exodus
15:11ff, where the Israelites sing of the victory God has
won them in bringing them out of Egypt: 'Who among
the gods is like you, O Lord? Who is like you . . . ?' The
text continues with a list of people who will fail to
prevail over God's people in war – Philistia, Moab, Edom
and Canaan. You see, it's the same song being sung to

different people. One to the emperor, one to God. One song is right and proper, one a travesty, a blasphemy, a song that should never be sung. But the comparison is helpful, because everyone understood that the emperor's power required obedience. Maybe he was the wrong guy to claim some of this stuff, but the obedience you should offer God then should be the same as the emperor asked for – if anything, stronger, more absolute, completely loyal.

The Roman Empire was a model to the first Christians of what the kingdom of God could be – but a negative, anti-model. All its claims and self-vaunting were the opposite of the real power of God, but they served as an example to the early Christians that complete sway was possible, and as a reminder that the only answer to the evil of Rome was the power of the one Lord God.

And this is an important idea – that something can be a help, a role model, an example *negatively* or by contrast with the thing it describes. The problem with using power images to describe God is that we use human images and then get hung up on the images rather than the truths they communicate. Some would argue against these ideas of complete fidelity and obedience to God, pointing out that calling Jesus 'Lord' may serve as a kind of religious justification in today's world for the human use of absolutist and anti-democratic power structures. 'Of course it is OK for me to force my people to do what I want. Isn't that God's way?' If God is like that then it's fine for us to be like that too. People will take advantage for their own ends.

Richard Bauckham disagrees. He writes: 'This is the exact opposite of the way the image of divine sovereignty functions in Revelation. There, so far from legitimising human autocracy, divine rule radically de-legitimises it. Absolute power, by definition, belongs only to God.'[1] That is to say, rather than power words that are used about God excusing the human forces that use the same power words, God's power completely opposes those who would claim it for themselves in an ungodly way.

Moreover, Bauckham points out that throughout the book of Revelation John is very careful not to reduce God to a human level: in chapter 4, there is one on the throne, but what does he look like? Like 'jasper and carnelian' (Revelation 4:3). In chapter 5 John is even careful about the way he describes Jesus, refusing to use a human physical picture: 'Then I saw a Lamb, looking as if it had been slain, standing in the centre of the throne' (Revelation 5:6). The point of this, Bauckham argues, is to show how different God is from us – to express his transcendence.

Real transcendence, of course, means that God transcends all creaturely existence. As the source, ground and goal of all creaturely existence, the infinite mystery on which all finite being depends, his relation to us is unique. We can express it only by using language and images in odd ways

---

1. Richard Bauckham, *Theology of the Book of Revelation* (Cambridge, 1993), p. 44.

that point beyond themselves to something quite incomparable with the creaturely sources of our language and images.[2]

In other words God is not like us but a bit better; he is completely other. The problem of language is that it is culturally bound to our existence here and now, so the way we use it to describe God will carry overtones we need to get beyond. The Roman context was the one in which the first Christians lived and understood about Jesus, so what we need to see is what was helpful to them, without foisting our own cultural hang-ups on them, or thinking them so simple as to be unable to get the power of an image without getting confused by that image.

When I say, 'I'm so hungry I could eat a horse,' you don't think I'm about to try to do that, do you? The image conveys the power of my hunger to you, but you are able to understand that I am speaking figuratively, not literally. I'm hungry, but I'm not able to eat a horse. Likewise, the early Christians called Jesus 'Lord', and the imperial reference was strong in that, but they did not think that Jesus would be like Nero, nor did they think that because Nero was called 'lord', he would be as good as Jesus. They did understand that lord Nero had to be obeyed; and the Lord Jesus had to be obeyed more.

2. *Ibid.*, pp. 44–45.

Roman society lived under an absolute 'omnipotent' ruler who used religious authority to make people obey. Despotism, tyranny, blasphemy and force show that system to be ungodly, but in doing so point towards God's total power, awesome in its extent, God's spiritual truth and purity, and a Christian's right desire to willingly serve and obey God alone. If we have no concept of total power, however warped the human version of that might be, then we lose something very precious that the early Christians had: an instinctive understanding that there is an absoluteness to God's power that changes our lives as we humbly submit. No submission, no recognising God's power; no recognising God's power, no radically changed people of God. Submission to God, total submission in worship – seeing him for who he is, us for who we are, and falling before him as a result – completely changes each Christian's heart.

It is in the kind of genuine worship that John portrays in his vision of heaven that we know ourselves to be finite creatures in relation to the transcendent mystery of God. False worship, such as John portrays in the worship of the beast, is false precisely because its object is not the transcendent mystery, but only the mystification of something finite.[3]

True worship is true when we worship the God who is completely above us, the one true God, and fall in obedience at his feet. False worship is false because it

---

3. *Ibid.*, p. 45.

makes a god out of something or someone that is not God.

The Roman context for 'Lord' helps us worship a mighty God, but we need more than this. We need to know who this mighty Lord is and what he is like if the word 'Lord' is to change our worship for good.

Holy, holy, holy is the Lord Almighty

The Roman picture of lordship enabled the early Christians to understand that God's rule was complete; that the Lord Jesus was to be submitted to, not argued with. But as we have seen, it gave a generally negative picture of what a lord was that could not possibly be the picture God wanted his people to have of him.

As I said earlier, this was corrected by the influence of Roman political government being interpreted through Jewish scriptural eyes. For here too we find a picture of power, though more often treated with alarmingly modern disrespect, but it is a power that possesses moral compassion and a desire to help the helpless, to stand up for the oppressed and to be involved with the ordinary lives of ordinary people. If we are to worship Jesus as Lord alongside our brothers and sisters of the first Christian centuries, understanding what they understood and being changed by the power of that understanding, singing words that have almost too much meaning, then to this Roman picture of power and obedience we must add the Jewish world of God's character and intervention.

It's like a song: there are words and there is music. Words give us understanding, but we say them once and move on. Said liturgies are often packed full of images and ideas, but we seldom have time to dwell on them, think about them, let them take a hold of us. Music warms our hearts, moves our emotions, makes us feel good, but a service of instrumental music alone would leave many people confused as to what had just happened. Words and music together give us understanding and the ability to respond to God emotionally, to take in ideas and to dwell on them, to say words of love and mean them. We need both.

The Jewish understanding of the word 'Lord' carries three main strands. As in Roman thought, it says that the Lord is all-powerful. Then it adds two new ideas. It speaks of his moral character – just what kind of God he is. And finally it speaks of a Lord who chooses to intervene on his people's behalf.

Now we've talked about power already, but there is an important addition the Jewish context gives. It's all about exclusivity. If God is Lord, and that Lord has complete power over all the earth and over all my life, there can only be one Lord. To have other lords popping up around the place is a contradiction in terms. It contradicts the unique nature of God, it denies that his power is absolute, it calls into question whether God is Lord at all.

In football terms, there is only one referee. He has assistants, but they don't run the game – the referee does. Now the crowd may think the ref is blind, but they don't run the game either. No matter how loud they shout, there is one referee, and he is not about to change his mind. Of course, the players feel they are in charge, but if they protest too much, they only run the risk of incurring the referee's wrath and receiving a yellow card. And managers, well, they feel a self-righteous indignation every time a referee dares to make a decision they disagree with, but they can't do anything about it. Everyone wants to run the game, but things go best when everyone accepts the man in black's decisions and the teams play on.

Of course, a referee at a football game is human and makes mistakes. That's not the point. The point is, there is one man in charge. Not 67,000, or however many people have turned up today to watch. Just so, there is one Lord. We all have opinions, but there is only one Lord. One God who sets the rules and gives us the power to live up to them. One judge. One.

We looked at the first commandment in Chapter 1, but let's have another quick reminder now: 'I am the Lord your God . . . You shall have no other gods before me' (Exodus 20:2–3). No other gods. There is just the one. And here we are not meant to let our minds wander to the question of whether other divine beings exist or not. 'Gods', as we have seen, can be anything we worship – anything we put in God's place. But an acceptance of other gods implies acceptance of their power. You don't put something in pole position in your life and give it no power. If the children come first, they rule you. Their whims and follies and joys and sicknesses take precedence over all your own needs. If it's a relationship that comes first, then that person becomes the recipient of your attention, your cash, your time, and their needs and desires rule you. If it's a career or an ambition, likewise. The things that come first rule us, have a power over us.

That power is rightly God's. And the people who would call him Lord and worship him must understand that power and live under it, and it alone. The word 'Lord' in our worship drives our hearts and minds to obeying that Lord completely. That is what the word means and requires. To call Jesus 'Lord', according to one German commentator, is to receive

> Unconditionally binding direction which gives meaning, measure and purpose to . . . life, and which demands an obedience that is not exhausted in elegiac cultivation of feeling but manifests itself in concrete action, especially towards others . . . 'We do and we hear' (Exodus 24:7) is the answer of those assembled on the mount of God as they receive the Law.[4]

If God is Lord, we do what he says. We take orders from nowhere else. And that doing somehow fulfils us in every way, especially as we seek to help others. Now this kind of obedience is what I call worship.

I know I'm taking time over this, but stick with me.

---

4. G. Quell, *Theological Dictionary of the New Testament* (Eerdmans, 1966), p. 1062, italics mine.

This word 'Lord' is so important in worship, in describing the risen Jesus whom we worship, because knowing what the word means has to make a difference to how we worship, to making us more biblical worshippers.

If there is one Lord, what is he like? Well, for a Jew, names are important. They mean something. Perhaps when you were at school you discovered what all the names in your class meant. For example, my name, Marcus, has to do with belonging to the Roman god of war, Mars. Now a Jewish child would be named in a way that described something of their character – just look up in Genesis why the patriarchs got their names to see how this works: Abraham, the father of many nations; Isaac, who made his parents laugh; Jacob, who swindled his brother out of a birthright but then became Israel, who struggled with God. I was not named Marcus because I have a war-like temperament (though I admit to an occasionally short fuse that might make the name seem more appropriate than I'd want it to be), but because my mum liked the name. That's how it tends to work in our society. We have a very different approach to names.

The word 'Lord' in the Old Testament, especially where Bibles print it as LORD in capitals, is a reference to the name of God, the unpronounceable YHWH, sometimes spelled out as Yahweh or Jehovah. For a Jew hearing the word 'Lord' in a religious context, the name of God and therefore the character of God comes straight to mind.

A name is therefore like a photograph. I have a photo

of my sister on my bedroom wall. She lives in Florida, and I don't get to see her that often. The photo is not there to remind me what she looks like in case I forget. It is there because every time I see it, I think about Gill – about what she's like: her kindness and generosity; her devotion to her son, Ben; the way she'd go out of her way to help someone; how she gets cross when she's tired. And I think about times we've shared together: fighting as kids; growing closer as we grew older; the dog she gave me; holidays in the sun. All sorts of things. That photo has a wealth of meanings, and every time I see it, they come to my mind.

A name, in Jewish thought, does all these things. It captures the essence of a person. So the word 'Lord' as the name of God captures his essence – if that were possible. It brings to mind all that he is and means to his people.

So what is God like, this Lord we worship? Here are a few starters:

The LORD, the LORD, the compassionate and gracious God, slow to anger, abounding in love and faithfulness, maintaining love to thousands, and forgiving wickedness, rebellion and sin. (Exodus 34:6–7)

The LORD is faithful to all his promises and loving towards all he has made. The LORD upholds all those who fall and lifts up all who are bowed down. The eyes of all look to you, and you give them their food at the proper time. You open your hand and satisfy the desires of every living thing. (Psalm 145:13–16)

The LORD is the everlasting God, the Creator of the ends of the earth. He will not grow tired or weary, and his understanding no-one can fathom. He gives strength to the weary and increases the power of the weak. (Isaiah 40:28–29)

Anyone who has seen me has seen the Father. (John 14:9)

I could go on and on painting this picture of God. I included that last quotation from John's Gospel because in it Jesus makes quite clear that he is just like the Father, and the Father is just like him. This is what God is like – Jesus. And every time we say that word 'Lord', or sing it in a song, it should carry all the weight of the character of the Jesus we worship and the Father who sent him. This word is our photo of Jesus, our picture of God. Again, I really believe we should be more thoughtful in the way we use it in our worship, for it carries so much with it, almost too much meaning for us to bear. It is the snapshot we keep with us in the wallet of our hearts, but it is worth far more than all the other treasures carried there added together.

And yet there is still more to this word 'Lord'. Where do we first encounter the word 'Lord' as the name of God in the Old Testament? In Exodus 3. At the end of chapter 2, the people cry out to God for help because of the slavery they have fallen into in Egypt. God hears their cry and in chapter 3 appears to Moses from the burning bush, and sets in action the plan that will lead to freedom.

In the midst of this encounter, Moses asks God what

he should say God's name is, if the Israelites ask him. God replies: 'I AM WHO I AM. This is what you are to say to the Israelites: "I AM has sent me to you"'(Exodus 3:14). The I AM stuff here is a reference to the YHWH name of God. The name literally means 'I am who I am'. It comes at this point in Israel's story because they needed God to intervene. We only have it because God got involved. And we keep getting it in the Old Testament because God keeps on getting involved – Moses, Joshua, the Judges, the Prophets, David, Solomon, Daniel, Nehemiah – all through the Old Testament God gets involved, and is worshipped as the LORD.

The name of the LORD is a concept of experience. It points to the ongoing historical encounter between God and his people. It is not just a list of inspiring character traits. It is that character with those traits in action in our lives. 'To call by the name of "Yahweh" is to confess and to be ready for encounter with this person.'[5] You don't dial 999 just to talk about the theory of crime, but because you need help right there and then. Similarly, you don't call on the name of the LORD because you are interested in the concept of a divinity, but because you expect to meet with him.

If there are a hundred people in a room with me and I hear someone call, 'Marcus!', I respond to them. This is because Marcus is a fairly uncommon name. I have known one or two other people with the same name over the last thirty years or so, but right now I don't

5. G. Quell, *Theological Dictionary of the New Testament*, p. 1063.

have any acquaintances who share my name. So if I'm at a railway station or in a supermarket and I hear someone call 'Marcus!' I'll still respond. You call my name, you get a response.

On the whole, I think it's fairly safe to say that God is better at responding to his name being called than I am to mine. To use his name is to expect to meet with him. To call out that word 'Lord' is to risk encounter.

We have needed to look at the character of this almighty Lord, because without knowing his character his power would be too scary for words. But now we see that this word 'Lord', when applied to God in the Jewish context of the time of the first Christians, does not simply rattle off a list of ideal qualities we would like to find in a God of total power, but tells us that this God is near and we can know and experience him for ourselves. Not distant, not separate, the word correctly understood says that this transcendent and utterly other God is right here, right now, with us and for us.

The book of Revelation slams this point home. Three times it refers to the Lord 'who was, and is, and is to come' (1:4, 8; 4:8). Now we have a great habit of seeing this as simply three tenses of the same thing – past, present and future. But if that were right, surely the third tense, the future option, would be different? Surely the future of 'was' and 'is' would come out as 'will be'? You know – 'He was here, he is here, he will be here.'

'Is to come' carries more with it. Not just a promise of future existence, God carrying on being God, but also the promise of future intervention – God carrying on being involved. Just as he came to help his people in the past – at the Passover, the Exodus, the cross – so he will come again to rescue the people who cry out to him. God the Lord, the self-defining God, names himself as one who will be involved with his people. Always. Yesterday, today and for ever. From beginning to end. Alpha to omega.[6]

My head hurts . . .

This has been a long walk down a complicated avenue. We have covered some major biblical ideas. Worship is the big picture, and the big ideas in Scripture are therefore full of things we need to know in order to worship better. This word 'Lord' is a key word. It is the Old Testament name of God, the word the Israelites used to worship God, and it became the title the early church chose for Jesus, a part of his name too, as they worshipped the one who had so recently walked with them.

It was a word their world knew well: some claimed it as their own – men who thought they could have ultimate power in every sphere of life over all people.

6. 'The biblical name of God YHWH was sometimes vocalised Yahoh and so transliterated into Greek (which has no consonant 'h') as IAΩ (iota, alpha, omega)' (Bauckham, *Theology of the Book of Revelation*, p. 27). Bauckham suggests that the alpha/omega references in Revelation may therefore be references to the word LORD.

Others saw in it the nature of God revealed; a snapshot of his character written down for us. And part of that character, that indescribable goodness and love, was the promise always to be involved in his people's lives. The Christians saw that this was right and that these qualities were now seen in Jesus, revealed and lived out in their own experience. This word 'Lord' had been made flesh, and had walked among them.

So now let's go back to the songs we started with. In the introduction I said that my working definition of worship was the entire Godward response of our lives, focused on the corporate church gathering. In our Sunday services we most clearly express the worship of our lives to our Lord Jesus, and for many of us it is those songs and hymns that provide the best vehicle for these acts of praise and adoration. But now, maybe, we have just gained something extra. We do not live in the same world as the people who gave us the words we use. Times change. Ideas move along. But if we understand what our ancestors in the faith meant when they gave us these words, then maybe their lives and faith still empower us to worship today. Are you ready?

> He is Lord, he is Lord.
> He is risen from the dead, and he is Lord.
> Every knee shall bow, every tongue confess
> That Jesus Christ is Lord.
>
> *Author unknown*

4

Free at Last

If an Inuit (Eskimo) from the Arctic circle were taken without any warning to the Sahara desert in the hottest part of the year, he would look out from his air-conditioned hotel room, see the brilliant sunshine and clear blue skies, then put on his thickest, furriest coat and boots before daring to open the door and step outside. It might seem strange to us, but to the Inuit the clear days – the days when the sun is brightest – are among the very coldest days. There will be no fresh snow because the temperature has plunged far below that level. So he sees the Saharan sun for the first time and judges it, wrongly, by his own experience.

The African tribesman who formed the other part of the exchange visit would find himself in a similar situation in the far north. The sky is blue, the sun low but clear, the sand appears strangely white. Obviously a hot day. He might have a cool shirt for protection against the burning sun, or he might just go out in very little at all. The surprise of the Arctic reality would if anything be more shocking than the Inuit's African experience.

Both characters, of course, find the world rewritten. The Inuit feels himself drowning in sweat because of the great heat, and the tribesman nearly freezes on the spot. What they have spent their whole lives learning – that certain skies mean certain weather – is desperately inadequate in the new situations surrounding them. If they are going to make a go of life in their new environments, they need to learn new responses, new reactions, new habits and new clothing customs pretty quickly!

When we come to faith as Christians, we are like that African in the Arctic. The world around us has just changed beyond all telling and we have to adapt ourselves to a whole new life. Everything has just turned itself the right way up, and every fibre of our being wants to swap it all back to the ways we used to know; the old ways, the comfortable, familiar ways. But it is not this new world we discover that needs changing; it is our hearts and wills that suddenly need to be retaught everything we thought we knew. The things that were at the heart of our lives have moved. The centre is now taken up by this God we have turned to. Too many times, Christians seem to reject the good things God gives and instead opt for as little difference as possible between their unconverted and redeemed lives. They are as daft as an Inuit in furs in the Sahara.

And the best of these good things God has for his people is worship. True worship. Wrong worship was what mucked the world up in the first place. We couldn't kick the habit, no matter how hard we tried, no matter how much help we were given. Then Jesus came and got it right – worship so perfect, so obedient, so true that it reversed the sin of the world and opened up heaven's door to us. The invitation before us is: will we come in and worship with him?

When John the Baptist is born, his father, Zechariah, after months of silence, sings out a song of praise to God. The point of the song is that God has done what he promised – redemption is coming, salvation is on its way, mercy is at the door, the oath sworn to Abraham is fulfilled. He is singing about what Jesus will accomplish, and the role this son of his, John, will have in pointing people to Jesus. What is fascinating for me is how Zechariah refers to the oath to Abraham, and how he interprets it. If you cast your mind or your eye back to Genesis and the Abraham story, you might think of people or land being the focus of God's promises to Abraham. But Zechariah sees things differently.

Zechariah, like Abraham, is an old man, and he sees the story from an old man's perspective. Abraham too has been promised a son – a son through whom all nations will be blessed. And now, having this son, he is told to take him up to Moriah and sacrifice him to God. He is told to worship God by offering up the most precious thing he has ever had: his dear son Isaac. Is it easy to think of his life's hope dashed by his own hands? No. It makes him terribly afraid. Yet God has requested it, and God will have it. Abraham goes, and the boy comes too, enjoying the trip, ignorant of its purpose. The old man is enthralled by fear, yet his obedience to God wins out. Perhaps it won't happen; perhaps God will provide an alternative sacrifice.

Then as Abraham raises his hand to slay his son, the Lord speaks. He blesses Abraham for his faith, provides a ram for the offering, and promises Abraham that all nations will be blessed through this son because of his obedience (Genesis 22). But what Zechariah sees here with the wisdom and insight of age is a different promise: he understands Abraham's fear. God is asking him too to give up his only son to be a prophet preparing the way for the Lord. But did God let Abraham down? No. Was Abraham wrong to give God everything? No. Did God provide for Abraham and Isaac? Yes. So should he, Zechariah, fear now that God has changed and will bring awful disaster on those who obey him? Of course not. For this is the oath God swore to Abraham – that we should be free to worship him without fear (Luke 1:74).[1] The elderly Abraham feared he would lose all, and God showed him that such fear was misplaced: obedience brings blessing, not disaster. We are free to worship God without fear. Zechariah sees the same promise. To worship and lose everything is hard when you're young, but there is time to rebuild, to do it all again; to worship and lose everything when you're old is harder. Except – this is the promise to

---

1. 'Serve' is an alternative reading to worship in the NIV. The ASB and now *Common Worship* use 'worship'.

Abraham, and God does not change – worshipping God never brings disaster; it always brings blessing; it frees us from fear; it gives us hope.

This is the new world we live in as Christians – a world where worship is no longer a minefield of rights and wrongs, and where we get it so wrong so often that sin leads to sin and God is further and further beyond our reach. Jesus has changed all that by his death on the cross, his perfect act of worship, and now he invites us to live in a different world, to worship without fear, to get right what we never thought we could.

Charlie was the first dog I had ever owned. We'd had animals as kids, but now this one was truly mine. He had been my sister's, but she was emigrating to the States, and she gave him to me. I loved him from the first. He was a wonderful Springer Spaniel, and became my best friend. But the first time Gill, my sister, came home from Florida, when I told Charlie to sit, he looked at Gill to see if he should. He was still her dog.

The second time she came back, however, it was a different story. When she told him to sit, he looked at me. And both my sister and I realised at that moment that Charlie had changed masters, and that meant his whole world had changed. A new allegiance meant a new life.

The life of worship

This in essence is the call of Romans 12: we have a new allegiance, a new Lord, and his worshipping death on the cross enables us to get right what we never thought we could. Paul puts the problem of the world's sin in worship terms in Romans 1. In Romans 3 he gives the solution in worship terms. Now in chapter 12 he calls his readers to live out the Christian life in worship terms.

> Therefore, I urge you, brothers, in view of God's mercy, to offer your bodies as living sacrifices, holy and pleasing to God – this is your spiritual act of worship. Do not conform any longer to the pattern of this world, but be transformed by the renewing of your mind. Then you will be able to test and approve what God's will is – his good, pleasing and perfect will. (Romans 12:1–2)

This has to be seen as a response to the first chapter of Romans. There, wrong worship led to wrong behaviour; here, right worship leads to right behaviour. There, such a shift from the wrong back to the right was impossible because of the way the whole of creation has been twisted by sin, but now, in the light of what Jesus has done, everything is different. In Tom Wright's words, 'Romans is all about the One God and what he has done – the appropriate response is to worship this God with the totality of self.'[2]

Let's spell it out, because this is our Christian lives we are talking about. If my first chapter focused on sin, and the second on the cross, then this is the third part of that argument: the Christian life as right worship lived

---

2. N. T. Wright, lecture 23 of 24 on Romans (Oxford University, 1990).

out in a wrong world – not just having a new song to sing, but singing that song with the whole of our lives. As Louie Giglio puts it, 'Our continual sacrifice of praise – our all-the-time expression of worship to God – takes two primary shapes. It's made up of words. *And deeds.*'[3]

In Romans 1, we have the 'wrath of God' being revealed against all the evil in the world. But in Romans 12 we see rather 'God's mercy' poured out on us. The pitch has changed. We have moved on because of Jesus, and his death on the cross. In Romans 1 people neither 'glorified . . . God nor gave thanks to him', but now in Romans 12 we offer ourselves 'holy and pleasing to God'; a right response from grateful people. Before, we were given over by God to the 'degrading of [our] bodies', and now we 'offer [our] bodies as living sacrifices'. We had 'a depraved mind' and now God gives us the 'renewing of [our] mind'. Once we 'did not think it worthwhile to retain the knowledge of God', but now we are 'able to test and approve what God's will is'. Everything is different to those who are in Christ Jesus.

But the *coup de grâce* is the bit I have left out. For all of this revolves around the concept of worship. The whole downward spiral had as its focus the idolatry and wrong worship of verses 22 to 25 of Romans 1: 'Although they claimed to be wise, they became fools and exchanged the glory of the immortal God for images made to look like mortal man and birds and animals

3. Louie Giglio, *The Air I Breathe*, p. 81, italics mine.

and reptiles . . . They exchanged the truth of God for a lie, and worshipped and served created things rather than the Creator.' Their worship was foolishness.

Paul describes Christian worship in 12:1 as 'spiritual' (or 'reasonable', as some translations put it). But the force of this word (*logikos* in the Greek) is to refute and replace all the folly of chapter 1: these people were senseless, engaging in worship that was nonsense. But now we offer worship that makes sense, as it finds its true object in the one true God. And just as wrong worship transformed the worshippers, made them less human, as they received the appropriate results of their worship choices, so worship that makes sense transforms the worshippers, making us more human, more in the image of the God who made us, more able to see and understand his ways. I might paraphrase the opening to Romans 12 in these terms: 'Therefore, because of everything God has done for us and the mercy he has shown us, we must offer our whole bodies as living sacrifices, the kind of worship that God loves, pure and just for him. This is worship that makes sense.'

Mike Thompson says, 'Humanity in Christ is called to do now what humanity originally failed to do – to offer what amounts to appropriate worship to the true God.'[4]

You see, before Paul can describe the moral dimen-

4. M. B. Thompson, 'Romans 12:1–2 and Paul's Vision for Worship', in M. Bockmuehl (ed.), *A Vision for the Church: Studies in Early Christian Ecclesiology in Honour of J. P. M. Sweet* (T. & T. Clark, 1997), pp. 121–32.

sion to the Christian life (how we should think and speak and behave), which he is going to do in the remainder of his letter to the Romans, he sets the basic rule. It is all about worship. How we act comes from how we worship. Just as in the past that meant wrong worship led to immoral acts, now right worship must lead to moral lives. Take worship out of that argument – reduce Christian living to simple morality – and you have missed the entire point. For Paul, there is no moral living, no being a good person, no doing the right thing apart from right worship: worship that makes sense, worship that involves us offering everything we have and are to the one true God through Jesus Christ his Son, in the power of the Holy Spirit.

It's like driving a car. You can indicate to pull out, you can use your rear-view mirror and wing mirror all you like, you can change gear flawlessly and have pedal work that is a beauty to behold. But it doesn't get you anywhere if the engine isn't switched on. Worship is the engine of the Christian life. All your good deeds and fine Bible teaching, all your evangelism and intercessory prayer, come from the worshipping heart. No worship, and they are worthless, because worshipping God remains command number one – the first, the root, the causal command. The rest of the Christian life comes from this command, this desire, this passion for worshipping God. When we worship God, we do what Jesus did on the cross. We enter into a whole new truth that turns the world the right way up, and suddenly we are back with our African friend in the Arctic. We have to learn to live life all over again, because true worship has just changed everything and we have got ourselves involved in an adventure that will blow our minds.

Worship changes life

On my last trip to Wengen I learned to ski. I'd had one or two outings previously on a dry ski slope in Llangranog in West Wales, but I'd never tried the real thing on snow. I was doing the chaplaincy with a couple of friends who were at that time training for ordained ministry in Cambridge. On the first day, our instructor, Karen, took James, Jon and me through the basics of starting and stopping, turning and traversing. It was a miserable day. The cloud was down, the snow was falling constantly and we could hardly see a thing. The second day was just the same, except Karen decided to push us and took us down a four-mile run. If you have ever experienced a white-out in the Alps you will know that everything loses perspective. All you can see is white. There are no shadows and there is no sense of depth or distance. Karen told us to follow her, to stay in her tracks. So we did. We must have completed that run in one of the slowest times in the history of the universe, but we did it and felt disproportionately pleased with ourselves.

The next day we were on our own. In order to boost our confidence, we decided to begin the day by doing the run Karen had shown us the day before. We knew we had done it once, so we could do it again.

The thing was, the weather had changed. Instead of cloud and constantly falling snow, there was blue sky, brilliant sunshine and views for miles all around in every direction. And as we began to ski, we began to see what we had done the day before, and stark disbelief set in. There was no way we could have done a slope that steep! Or a track that narrow! Or any of a number of seemingly impossibly difficult parts of this particular run. Vertigo gripped me. Somebody once told me that vertigo is not the fear of heights so much as the fear of throwing yourself off heights. Well, as I looked down the slope before me I thought, 'No wonder I've got vertigo. All we ever do is throw ourselves off mountains and hope for the best!' When we couldn't see, we followed Karen. When we could see, we panicked.

Worship, in life, is like following Karen. There are things we don't understand, things we can't grasp, things beyond our power to control, but if we keep our eyes on Jesus, if we worship him, keeping him at the centre of our vision, following his tracks, then we will make it to the end. He will guide us on the best paths, but we only see them if we follow him, if we keep our eyes and our hearts fixed on him. Let's think carefully about what I'm saying here: worshipping God is the point of conversion (from worshipping anything and everything else) – the reason we have been saved from the sin of wrong worship is to engage in the blessings of right worship. As George Bush Snr is reputed to have said, 'The main thing is to keep the main thing the main thing.' But as we worship Jesus, as we follow him, giving our hearts and souls and minds to him in adoration and praise, other things begin to happen to us.

In Chapter 1 we looked at the first four of the Ten Commandments, noting that they are all about our worship relationship with God. Now we need to look at the rest of the Ten Commandments, because with our worship sorted, there are huge implications for the rest of life. With our eyes set on following Jesus, keeping the main thing the main thing, this priority of worship inevitably and rightly sets the agenda for everything else.

When the worship of God by the Spirit of God is made the glorious first priority in our lives – the worship of a God who loves all people – then we too must love all people. This must start with those closest to us, even when they fail to understand us, even when we feel we are right and they are wrong, and loving them means respecting them always no matter what. This is the essence of the fifth commandment.

When the worship of God by the Spirit of God is made the glorious first priority in our lives – the worship of a God who gives life to all and new life to all who ask – then we must treasure the gift of life, and nurture it in all. This is the sixth commandment.

When the worship of God by the Spirit of God is made the glorious first priority in our lives – the worship of a God who is always faithful and true – we too must be faithful and true, in all our relationships. This is the seventh commandment.

When the worship of God by the Spirit of God is

made the glorious first priority in our lives – the worship of a God who gifts his people with all they need and much more beside – we must learn the art of Christian contentment, and hold the things of this world on open palms, not seeking to grab what we can, but to trust the great Giver. This is the eighth commandment.

When the worship of God by the Spirit of God is made the glorious first priority in our lives – the worship of a God whose words are the stuff of truth – we must speak his language of truth always and everywhere. This is the ninth commandment.

When the worship of God by the Spirit of God is made the glorious first priority in our lives – the worship of a God who has promised to be with us, caring and providing – we must act on this faith, not trapped in the envy of others, but wonderfully released by the generosity of God. This is the tenth commandment.

Worship comes first

Let's remind ourselves of the ground we have covered here. The Ten Commandments show that the point of life is worshipping God, and from that comes all moral and social behaviour. Love God first, then love your neighbour. Paul's argument then comes into play: sin is fundamentally about getting worship wrong; Jesus' death on the cross is presented as the perfect worship that overcomes this sin and opens up the way for us to follow by faith. And as we believe and trust in Jesus and what he has done for us, we are freed to worship without fear, to get right what we never thought we could, to live as God intended, loving and worshipping him in righteousness, which is simply a right relationship with God. Even more than that, this right behaviour that comes from our right relationship with God, which comes from our worship of God, is in itself worship; because this too is our response to God.

A. W. Tozer puts this in his usual succinct way: 'Jesus was born of a virgin, suffered under Pontius Pilate, died on the cross and rose from the grave to make worshippers out of rebels! He has done it all through grace. We are the recipients.'[5] Or again: 'We are brought to God and to faith and to salvation that we might worship and adore him . . . that we might be, individually and personally, vibrant children of God, loving God with all our hearts and worshipping him in the beauty of holiness.'[6] We have been made Christians that we might worship Christ. It's as simple as that.

But all along I've been carrying a specific definition of worship – the entire Godward response of our lives, focused in corporate expression. That is to say, not just singing the songs (but including singing the songs) and not just living the life (but including living the life). So when I say that the entire point of our salvation is that we might worship God, it is not my intention you should hear me say, 'Jesus died on a cross so we can

5. A. W. Tozer, *Whatever Happened to Worship?* (Kingsway, 1986),
   p. 13.
6. *Ibid.*, p. 15.

sing "Majesty".' There's more to worship than that.

My piano teacher would sometimes set me a piece to learn, and when I came back a week later he would listen to it, pull a face and say, 'Play it like this.' Then he would play it for me. After he had finished, I took my place back at the piano and played it again, but this time I would imitate my teacher, using his emphasis, playing like him, with his feeling and timing. My playing became like his, and in that process I became a far better pianist. Sometimes he would stop me, surprised at the accuracy of my imitation of his playing, and ask me how I did it. The answer was simple: I listened to him, and as I listened to him I understood what the music was about, and as I understood, I could do it too.

So in worship we listen to the Lord, we hear life played well, and hearing it we find we can play better ourselves. Christopher Cocksworth puts it this way: 'By glorifying God, we are glorified because we are becoming what we have been created to be.'[7] Now there is an important dynamic here: we are created to worship God, and when we do this thing we were created for, something changes in us, makes us more complete, more human, more than we were, because doing this thing means we are becoming what we are meant to be.

When I first began to lead worship in church, I was

---

7. C. Cocksworth, *Holy Holy Holy* (Darton, Longman & Todd, 1997) p. 146.

terrified. How could I get all these people to worship
Jesus, rather than just look at me and think I'm no good
at this job? A friend prayed with me and told me to
relate to God in public just as I would do at home. He
was the same. I was the same. Sure, all these people
weren't normally there at home, but you can't have
everything. And as I started to lead, an image came into
my mind of a fish in water. Just a fish. In water. Hardly
the most profound thing. Except it was exactly how I
felt. Suddenly, from being terrified by the enormity of
the task facing me, a task I'd avoided for years, I felt like
a fish in water. In my element. Doing what I was made
to do.

This sense of extraordinary well-being began to regularly affect me whether I was leading worship or being
led by somebody else. Just worshipping Jesus would do
it. Not always, I have to say, but often. And it began to
make an impact on my life generally. When you start
the day by making the choice to worship Jesus, it makes
a difference, because the worship choice makes a moral
choice. The songs sung and the Lord encountered
require a certain life to be lived out. For the worship to
be real, the rest of the day has to be affected by that
first half an hour. And even if, being slow, stupid and
occasionally stubborn, the life I have lived has not
matched the songs I have sung and the prayers I have
prayed step for step, the songs and the prayers have
lifted my life beyond what was possible before.

This is the other side of the worship coin. I really
mean that worshipping Jesus is the point of life. And

how we worship leads to how we act. A half-hearted
worship life will lead to half-hearted Christian living. You
want a gospel lifestyle? Get worshipping God. Why?
Because 'Christian worship is an ongoing process of
commitment to Jesus and to his values. It is also an
ongoing exposure to the Spirit who empowered him so
that we may be equipped to live his life and to work for
his values.'[8] Singing and praying 'Jesus is Lord' (or words
like it) every day means that every day we sign up to
worshipping the one true God. Worshipping the one
true God every day opens us up to his Spirit, and this
Spirit gives us the power and the grace we need to go
on and daily live a life that matches the words, a life
that too may be called 'worship'. That is why
commandments five to ten follow without break from
one to four. That's why Romans 13 to 15 follows from
chapter 12. It's all part of the great scheme of God: we
are to worship him in everything, in all our songs and
sermons, and in all our daily living too.

The second part of this book will be an exploration of
how this pattern of worship and living works together,
taking worship encounters in Matthew's Gospel as a
starting point. But before I get there, I want to look at
two views on how this dynamic actually works itself out
in the history of the church.

---

8. *Ibid.*, p. 206.

The early church example

Alan Kreider, in his little booklet *Worship and Evangelism in Pre-Christendom*,[9] argues that the strength of the early church's stand against the attacks of paganism lay in its worship. Time and again, churches had every reason to fall by the way in a society that opposed so much of what they stood for. And yet these churches grew, and membership increased in a world where from time to time just belonging meant you could lose your job or even your life. Several professions had their own gods and religious rites. Being a Christian meant promising not to be involved with these. The classic would be the armed services.

Now Christian worship drew people into the church not because they came to a service and liked the music; indeed pagans were banned from attending services at all. If you expressed a desire to become a convert, eventually you would be invited to attend the first part of worship, but never the communion – not till you were baptised at the end of a long period of training for Christian living. So how did worship draw people in? It changed those who went:

It performed the function of re-forming those pagans who joined the church into Christians, into distinctive people who lived in a way that was recognisably in the tradition of

9. A. Kreider, *Worship and Evangelism in Pre-Christendom* (Grove Books, 1995).

Jesus Christ. As such these people, re-formed, would be attractive. And not only attractive but free . . . This . . . was good news, news that was new.[10]

People who worshipped Jesus became different people, better people. The difference, the improvement, drew others in to find out why their friends had changed.

This was because throughout the worshipping life of the church, enormous emphasis was put on consistency, on words and deeds living up to each other. If they were a body, they had to have a distinctive common life, a visible bond between members that the world could see. If they loved each other, then the holy kiss in communion had to be genuine – restoring relationships where needed, but never a pretence that all was well when in reality it wasn't. Prayer was seen as invalid if a member held anything against another believer. Sacraments were pointless if they did not empower changed lives. Teaching was futile if not lived out. As we go on later in this book to look at some of the lessons on worship that Matthew draws in his Gospel, we shall see that this emphasis on words and deeds matching each other was something Jesus repeatedly taught. For now, here are some examples of the standards the second- and third-century Christians set themselves.

Those who bear anger and malice towards their brethren, God does not hear; and though you pray three times in

10. *Ibid.*, ch. 4.

one hour you shall gain nothing, for you are not heard by reason of your enmity against your brother.[11]

It is of small account to be baptised and receive the Eucharist, unless one profit by it in both deeds and works.[12]

When for instance they hear from us that God says, 'It is no credit to you if you love those who love you, but it is to your credit if you love your enemies and those who hate you,' when they hear these things they are amazed at such surpassing goodness. But when they see that we fail to love not only those who hate us, but even those who love us, then they mock at us and scoff at the Name.[13]

Kreider finishes his book with a plea that today's church rediscover the power of integrated worship – worship that makes a difference, where we understand and mean the words we say and sing, and put them all into practice; where the reason we are converted reaches out to convert others:

Christianity will rather survive because God's Spirit is enabling Christians to worship so they will live, not as mere residents but as in early centuries, as resident aliens, imaginative disciples of Jesus who are purveyors of good

---

11. Didascalia Apostolorum 2.53, quoted in *Ibid.*, ch. 17.
12. Cyprian, ad Quirinum 3.26, quoted in *Ibid.*, ch. 18.
13. 2 Clement 13, 3–4, quoted in *Ibid.*, ch. 19.

news to our time. I believe that worship can nurture people today, as it nurtured the pre-Christendom Christians, to be missionaries to our culture.[14]

The contemporary example

Don't get the wrong idea. I'm not saying for a moment that Christian worship today misses the mark and fails to change people into the people they should be. Though of course I do believe that job could be more effectively carried out by a church that really understood and warmed to the task. But in fact I think God is better at his job than we often give him credit for. When we worship him, he changes us, even if sometimes we are completely ignorant of what is going on or why.

When you spend time in the sun, you tan (or burn!) with no effort at all. You don't think about it – it just happens. When you go swimming you get wet. Getting wet probably wasn't the purpose of the swim – you just wanted to exercise – but it just happened. You did one thing, and got something else into the bargain.

Professor Robin Gill is a theologian whose speciality is the study of Christian ethics: the morals that shape the way we choose to live. Now he is quite clear that ethics or morals or how we live is not the point of worship ('Most practising . . . Christians . . . would appear rather to hold that the principal object of liturgy is to worship God. Values that are generated in this process are a

14. *Ibid.*, ch. 25.

consequence of worship and not its object'[15]), but worship does shape the values we live by. It is a simple theory: if we worship a God who cares, then surely we will feel it right to go out and care for others. If the most important person in life, and for the Christian that ought to be God, is shown to be on the side of the poor, the oppressed, the prisoner, the blind, the sick, the weary, the lost . . . then given that we have signed up to this God's values and priorities by deciding to worship him, it is only natural that we too should be on the side of the poor, the oppressed, the prisoner, the blind, the sick, the weary, the lost.

Gill puts it this way:

> Individuals who believe in theory that there is a God who cares (and who encourages them to care) are confronted in worship with this caring God. In worship we are invited to open our hearts and minds to the presence of God and then to ask God, in turn, to shape these hearts and minds . . . Within worship moral values take on a more demanding and insistent shape than they do outside worship; they change the very way we see the world. And worship itself becomes a form of care, requiring that we should go out to help the world to become more God-like.[16]

Where is the evidence for this? Well, historically we

15. Robin Gill, *Moral Communities* (University of Exeter Press, 1982), p. 67.
16. *Ibid.*, p. 81.

might cast our minds back to achievements such as the abolition of slavery or the ending of child labour and find important Christian people sponsoring these movements. We might look to the aid and relief agencies currently tending to any number of human disasters worldwide and see what proportion are linked to the faith of the caring God. Gill takes two studies by the European Value Systems group in 1981 and 1990, and finds a series of encouraging statistics. In the community at large, 9 per cent of people go to church at least once a week, and 51 per cent practically never show up. But among those involved in unpaid voluntary work, 27 per cent go to church once a week or more, and only 30 per cent never show. But even more remarkable is that among committed Christians, almost half are involved in some form of voluntary work; among those who profess no religious faith at all that figure slips to just 10 per cent.[17]

People who worship, care. People who love God love their neighbour. People who have their lives turned the right way up really live. People who worship God find themselves changed by this worship. This was never supposed to be the focus ('Let's worship God so that we can be nicer people'); it was meant just to be a response of love to the God who is love. But his love proves even greater than we expected, because we are changed, made better, made more completely human as we worship him and find ourselves made like him. Re-

17. *Ibid.*, p. 19.

made. Re-created. Turned the right way up, and therefore turning the right way up as much of the world
around us as we can.

Worship is the big picture. It is the song of our salvation. The whole Christian story is told in the Bible in
terms of worship. Sin, the cross, salvation – these are
primarily worship issues. Worshipping God is what life is
meant to be about, and as we commit ourselves to it,
we and all the world with us are changed for good as
that worship seeps out from the 'religious' bit of life to
the whole story.

In the remaining chapters of this book we are going
to look at Matthew's Gospel, and see how this was
always meant to be.

PART TWO:

WORSHIPPING JESUS

The Kiss of Worship

Most of us watch at least one soap opera on TV. The one I like, I have to confess, is *Neighbours*. I wish I could claim it was the street cred of *Eastenders* or the social comedy of *Coronation Street*; but no, just comfortable old *Neighbours*. These strange Australians have been invading my house daily for so many years I can't remember a time without them. From Mrs Mangel to the Scullies, there have been so many characters I have known so much about. Saintly Helen, for example, who was the perfect counsellor to the problems of others, yet every time she let a man into her life we all cried out, 'Stop! Stop now! Don't you know he's a conman/liar/two-faced cheat?' (delete as appropriate). Or if he was a decent chap, then we hung our heads and waited for him to die. Horribly. But soon.

We hear stories of people who watch these characters and forget that they are only characters in a TV show.

People send them birthday cards, but not on the actors' birthdays, on the characters'. Wedding cakes, condolences after a bereavement and even death threats all come flooding into the studios where the shows are made. And we smile little smiles to ourselves and wonder how people could be so gullible. Then we switch on today's episode and laugh and cry with our fictional friends.

And if by some chance we meet one of the actors in real life, the most disconcerting thing is that they don't know us. Surely you've had the experience of seeing someone and being on the verge of going over and greeting them warmly and asking them how they are, when suddenly (just in time) it clicks: they don't know you. It's Libby Kennedy or Dot Cotton or Mike Baldwin. You recognise them and know them from the TV, but you've never met. However familiar you find that face, the person who wears it is in fact a stranger. And even if they have been in your house every day for decades, they don't know it. It is just a TV show – quite literally a trick of the light.

I've never met a soap star by accident, but I once went to the opera, and this very tall thin chap sat in front of me. I knew I knew him, but I could not for the life of me think of his name. So I racked my brain. Did I know him from college? No, I thought not. Was he from some band I'd been in? No, I didn't think so. Was he a friend of a friend I'd met at some church do? That didn't seem right. Then suddenly it clicked. I recognised him, but he didn't know me. Sitting in front of me was

Tony Adams of Arsenal and England.

In a world where the most famous people on the planet are the entertainers we welcome into our homes on the TV, on video, on CD or on the radio, sometimes we need to stop and do a reality check on our worship. For God is not the star of an eternal soap opera that we traipse out to see in the discomfort of church every Sunday morning. No, this works the other way round. Sometimes we act towards God as we would towards Tony Adams: if we were to see him, we'd remember just in time he doesn't actually know us. It's just that we sit and watch him with thousands of others up and down the country on the same day every week.

But Jesus is not just a character in a nice story. He is reality – so real that worshipping him changes our lives. And as we worship him we realise how near he is to us. 'God is presence; here now, real, a person, loving, acting. He is not the Great Absent One. Nor is he the God of yesterday who was present in power to the early church and yet leaves us . . . to simply grit our teeth and believe that God is around someplace.'[1] There is a relationship here between us and God, and it is not make-believe, it is not gullibility, it is not to be pitied in others. Rather it is to be aimed for in our own lives.

Worship is the mainstay of that relationship as we appreciate who we are in the sight of God. We fall before him because he is greater than we are. But we

1. K. McDonnell (ed.), *Presence Power and Praise: Documents on the Charismatic Movement* (Collegeville, 1980).

do not fall before one who does not know us. He knows. He cares. And in his mercy, as we come to him in worship, so he comes to us. Robin Green puts it this way:

> Worship and liturgy care for us. God, through them, pays loving attention to us and we in turn are able to express the whole of our human experience to God. Worship is able by its very nature to touch some of the deepest springs of the human psyche and to help us to face those sides of our self that we dare not face. Pastoral insights are able to help us understand the complex needs and hopes that we bring to worship. Without them . . . there is a real risk that liturgy will become increasingly archaic and sterile. But if we can connect our worship and our pastoral care many fruitful areas of renewal and change will be opened up.[2]

That is to say, as we worship the God who cares, we are cared for, and church life in general would be the better for people seeing and making use of this link more often.

It is a simple link to make, especially when we consider the most frequently used word for worship in the New Testament: the Greek word *proskuneo*,[3] which in itself speaks of encounter with God, and in the way it

---

2. Robin Green, *Only Connect* (Darton, Longman & Todd, 1987), pp. 2–3.

3. A full discussion of this word and its meanings can be found in the Appendix.

is used in the New Testament speaks of encounters that always make a difference. From here on, we are going to look at the encounter of worship, and the difference it makes to us. We are going to see how we are supposed to meet with Jesus in person as we worship – a person we recognise and know, and who also knows us; not a make-believe character or a superstar off the TV, but our own, very real, Lord.

A Gospel of worship

We will be taking a detailed look at Matthew's Gospel, because it has a lot to say about worship. In all, Matthew has ten stories, ten events or parables where *proskuneo* worship makes a difference. Interestingly, Mark includes five of these stories in his Gospel. Yet he does not attach the word *proskuneo* to any of them. Could it be that, inspired by the Holy Spirit, Matthew really is trying to get us to see something special here? Could it be that he has a special point to make, a special emphasis he wants the churches to which he is writing to understand? Could it be that this issue of worship is one he wants his churches to see in every page of his Gospel as they find it on every page of their lives together?

Because what are we doing here? We are trying to see how worshipping God is the big picture of our Christian faith. We are trying to see how the big picture is made up of the big ideas – ideas like sin and the cross and the Christian life; ideas we know well but don't put into a worship context often enough. So far we've done this largely by following the structure of Paul's letter to the Romans, one of the big places of Scripture. But now we will move on to see how these things are held together in Matthew's Gospel, to demonstrate that this whole idea is indeed a major biblical concept. We need to see that what Paul writes about is the same thing as those who travelled with Jesus wrote about – that what is true in the gospel is true in the Gospels.

5

O Worship the King

Back in May 1999, when Manchester United won the European Cup Final, the city of Manchester went mad. There were street celebrations that lasted through the night as those who had been unable to travel to Spain rejoiced in their own city. When the team got back to Britain, there was an open-top bus tour through the streets of Manchester, watched by thousands in person and millions on TV. Here were the Champions, riding home in victory. The year after, United did not take part in the FA Cup. They were knocked out of the European Cup at the quarter-final stage, and had to settle for 'just' winning the Premiership. There was no party in the city, no civic reception, no bus tour. For the last few games of the season, it seemed as if half the team had already started their summer holidays, and those left behind took it easy and cantered home to finish the season with eleven consecutive victories.[1]

Now, if you are not a United fan but are still reading, let me explain why I'm rehearsing these facts with you. You see, the morning after the last day of that 1999–2000 season, a year after United's European win, *The Times* newspaper revealed that there would be a city-wide celebration to mark the previous day's results. But the city celebrating this time was Bradford, not Manchester.

> The City of Bradford will today stage the first civic reception for a team finishing seventeenth in the FA Carling Premiership. The players of the team that escaped relegation on the last day of the season, who have been in the bottom three for much of the past eight months, will ride into the city centre in an open-top bus, and not one single person, fanatic or neutral . . . will begrudge them their celebration.[2]

On the day after the football season finished, a team that had just avoided being thrown out of the top flight of English football celebrated like champions, and the champions were as quiet as a team that had just escaped relegation. Bradford City paraded like winners, and Manchester United were nowhere to be seen. Anyone watching the two teams, and not knowing the reality of their results, would have been forgiven for

---

1. OK, so I'm a fan, but you enjoy your team's successes too!
2. Oliver Holt, *The Times*, 15th May 2000.

mistaking the champions for also-rans, and the lucky relegation escapees for champions.

The very first worship story we find in Matthew's Gospel takes up this idea (2:1–12). It is about what things look like and how they really are. It concerns a man who looks like a king. He has all the trappings, and many people are fooled by him, but he finds himself ignored by wise men from the East searching for the true King. Instead, they go on to find a new-born baby in a village in the middle of nowhere, but they know that despite appearances, this one is the real thing. A real King. *The* true King, with real power given by God, not pretend power given by an invading army, a King with real authority, who will reign for ever. The wise men are not fooled by a party thrown by an also-ran; they see through the fizz and fancy labelling, and find real kingship hidden in a cellar, in an unmarked bottle.

The wise men come towards the Promised Land to kiss God's promised Messiah, and Herod is scared. He understands their desire and it makes him afraid. These wise men come asking for a King of the Jews, so that they might worship him. Well, Herod is king in the land of the Jews, but these visitors do not worship him. So they are after more than another king. They are after God's King, the Messiah. Only he would be worth such a trip. 'Is it possible?' he asks his advisers. 'Is it possible that there should be a new King of the Jews? A real one? And where would he be born?'

He gets his answer, and decides to use these visitors from the East to help him. He sends them to Bethlehem, but asks them to return when they have found him so that he may follow in their footsteps; make his own pilgrimage and worship the child.

The Magi go. They find mother and child in a house in Bethlehem and they bow down and worship Jesus. They give their gifts fit for a King and a priest, and then depart. But they don't return to Herod, having been warned in a dream to use a different route. Good thing too, for Herod's definition of worship is radically different from the Magi's. The gift he brings is the sword, his kiss is deadly, his homage is homicide – or rather infanticide, as all the boys under two in the region of Bethlehem are slaughtered.

Matthew presents here two very different attitudes; two very different hearts on display. One is superficially splendid, but beneath the surface is deceptive, unwilling to look for itself, and longs to preserve life exactly as it is. The other is genuine, has travelled far and longs to see the promise of God revealed. One looks right; the other *is* right.

So the first question we are faced with is stark and simple: what is the intent of these worshippers? And which attitude is more like our worship?

Matthew does not make it hard for us to see the right answer. He wants us, however, to see the question, because actually it is all too easy to slip into wrong attitudes, and contrasting the two helps us make good choices. So much of Matthew's teaching throughout his Gospel takes the form of contrasts: a right example and a wrong one. Just as he establishes the theme of worship that will run through the entire book here at the start, he establishes his method of offering alternative reactions – one right, one not.

You see, I expect that if I sat down and asked any member of any church I have ever been in whether they had the attitude of Herod or that of the Magi when it came to worship, they would want to answer 'The Magi', without exception. But I think the answer might not be so easy after a little more reflection.

Here are two choices: do we come to church on Sunday in order to give or to get? To give away everything we have, trusting the Lord with our whole life – family, wallet, job, hopes, ambitions, the lot – without a thought of any return? After all, the Magi certainly did not file an expenses claim for their trip. Or do we come to get fulfilment, teaching, enjoyment, friendship, our needs attended to? I'm not saying that these are all bad things. Far from it. But Matthew says that the attitude they come with needs attention, and may indeed be 'bad'. In worship we are encouraged to make good choices, because worship is the place where we meet Jesus, and in his presence we should be free to choose what is right, even if what is right is also a little scary.

I think that most of us unchallenged often come with the second attitude – to get what we want – and our worship allows us that choice: to choose what is easy rather than what is right. But it should not be so. We should face ourselves with some reality, some tough issues, and in our worship learn how to make right choices by the examples set before us, so that when we leave the worship gathering we are more equipped to make right choices in life.

When I trained for ordination in Oxford, it seemed I was constantly surrounded by students facing hard choices. Some of their most frequently asked questions were: Should I go out with this person? Should I take this course option? Should I apply for this job? Actually, as an aside, when it comes to the 'What do I do with my life?' issues, I always feel that God is probably more interested in the way we live than the way we make a living.

So how does worship help us make the choices we face day by day? Does it simply take us out of life for an hour of escapism before the hard realities bite back, or does it in fact teach us how to face reality with all its complex choices and deal with these choices in a Christian way?

You see, to go back to the story I began this chapter with, for all the vibrancy of the party, Bradford City's celebrations in early summer 2000 were only a moment's break from reality. Nothing had changed. They hadn't gone down a division, but nor had they become safe where they were. The next season found them suffering all the same problems, fighting all the same battles. A big party did not make them Championship contenders. And neither must worship be simply a party that masks hard realities. Worship in spirit and in truth must make us face the truth, the hard realities, the tough choices, but face them in the light of the Holy Spirit, who shows us the truth about Jesus. If we party and ignore the truth, we perish, but if we seek the truth through our worship, God changes everything. Writing about John in the book of Revelation, Christopher Cocksworth points out, 'While he was worshipping in the Spirit, he encountered the person of Christ, and was then taken before the presence of God to see things as they really were.'[3]

Matthew's Gospel is good news for people facing hard choices. And his emphasis on worship helps us look at these choices in the midst and in the light of our worship, and to live out our responses *as* worship.

All hail King Jesus?

Of course, the contrast we have here in Matthew 2 is all about two kings – Jesus and Herod – one real, one false. And with this contrast, the issue of right and wrong worship (whom will you serve?) begins to hit home practically. We've dealt with it theoretically in the earlier chapters of this book, but now we must see the rubber hitting the road.

The wise men come to worship the King of the Jews, but in Jerusalem they do not see anyone matching their expectations – certainly not Herod. What makes the infant Jesus so different as a king? Perhaps this can best be illustrated by reference to that other Herod, the one who beheaded John the Baptist.

We move forward 30 or so years to the time of Jesus'

3. C. Cocksworth, *Holy Holy Holy*, p.81.

public ministry, to the events recorded in chapter 14 of Matthew's Gospel. Now Matthew tells us several stories that link the ideas of kingship and worship. He is laying very careful ground so that we make the simple link that whatever we worship rules us. And that can be good or bad, so we need to choose wisely, and when it comes to people worth worshipping because they rule well, Jesus is head and shoulders above the available alternatives.

Let's look at Matthew 14, which begins with two kingship stories. For in the accounts of the beheading of John the Baptist and then the feeding of the five thousand, Matthew compares and contrasts the one who is called king and lives in a palace but has little care for God's people, with God's true King, who lovingly exercises God's reign over his people. I think I can show the contrast best by lining up these two stories next to each other, so we can clearly see what Matthew is showing us. The table on pp.128–9 demonstrates this, and the column in the middle is simply a brief comment to show how the two passages work together.

One of these men, Herod, has the title of 'king', but fails to live up to all that this entails. He imprisons John for daring to speak truths he does not want spoken; he creates the afflicted with no one to help, rather than helping him. He takes no pity but sends this needy man needlessly to his death, for he cares nothing for an innocent man's blood if his own reputation is in question.

Jesus is different. The crowd have no one to help them, so he takes centre stage to come to their relief. He has compassion for them and provides for their needs so they may live. Here is a description of how God's King should act from the Psalms: 'He will deliver the needy who cry out, the afflicted who have no-one to help. He will take pity on the weak and the needy and save the needy from death. He will rescue them from oppression and violence, for precious is their blood in his sight' (Psalm 72:12–14). Ultimately, of course, the bread that Jesus blesses, breaks and gives for others will become a symbol of how he cares so much for the people's blood that he will give his own body and blood that they might be delivered from the ultimate oppression and violence of sin and death. The people understood at least part of all this at the time because John's Gospel makes it quite clear that after the miracle of the feeding of the five thousand (John 6:15) they wanted to make Jesus king by force.

So here are Matthew's two pictures of kingship: weakness, unfaithfulness and cowardice; or strength, compassion and life-giving good. And the worship issue is: whom will you follow? The real King, the one who is everything he ought to be, everything we ever hoped for, or a false idol who can't deliver. One who turns the tide of humanity, or one who is swayed by whims and oaths and saving face?

Think of it in terms of lordship. What do we have here in Matthew's Gospel but the very same issues – the power of God, the character of God and the intervention of God in our lives in our favour? Herod rules without being in power; his character is deeply flawed. And although clearly he intervenes in John's life,

1. At that time Herod the tetrarch heard the reports about Jesus . . .	*time*	13. When Jesus heard what had happened
2. 'This is John the Baptist . . . risen from the dead! That is why miraculous powers are at work in him.'	*wonders*	14. When Jesus landed and saw a large crowd, he had compassion on them and healed their sick.
3. Now Herod had arrested John and bound him and put him in prison	*time*	15. As evening approached
4. for John had been saying to him: 'It is not lawful for you to have her.'	*problem*	15. the disciples came to him and said, 'This is a remote place, and it's already getting late . . .'
5. Herod wanted to kill John, but he was afraid of the people	*wrong solution*	15. Send the crowds away, so that they can go to the villages and buy themselves some food.'
7. he promised with an oath to give her whatever she asked.	*king's solution*	16. Jesus replied, 'They do not need to go away. You give them something to eat.'

8. 'Give me here on a platter the head of John the Baptist.'

9. The king was distressed, but because of his oaths and his dinner guests, he ordered that her request be granted

10. and had John beheaded in the prison.

11. His head was brought in on a platter and given to the girl, who carried it to her mother.

12. John's disciples came and took his body and buried it.

17. 'We have here only five loaves of bread and two fish,' they answered.

challenge

18. 'Bring them here to me,' he said. And he directed the people to sit down on the grass.

king's response

19. Taking the five loaves and the two fish and looking up to heaven, he gave thanks and broke the loaves.

action

19. Then he gave them to the disciples, and the disciples gave them to the people.

challenge met

20. They all ate and were satisfied, and the disciples picked up twelve basketfuls of broken pieces that were left over.

aftermath

one can hardly see it as a positive encounter. But Jesus makes the grade. When the disciples panic, Jesus uses his power to provide for all. He cares, he gives, and his character is truly what one would expect from God. His intervention is all about providing for others, and more than providing – there are after all twelve baskets of left-overs.

The Magi in chapter 2 prove themselves wise men by their discernment on this issue. Their Herod is every bit as false a king of God's people as John the Baptist's Herod. They are right not to bow in worship to him. They make the right choice. Matthew is keen that we see their choice – and make it with them.

Let me join a few more dots together so we can see the whole picture that bit more clearly. In contrasting Herod the Great and the infant Jesus, and then the later Herod and the adult Jesus, Matthew is writing a series of comparisons between false kingship and legitimate kingship. Between a false king and the true King.

And forgive me the obvious question, but who is the true King? Like good Sunday school children we reply, 'Jesus.' OK, but let's push that a bit further. In 1 Samuel 8 the Israelites ask God for a human king, and God says that in making this request the people have rejected him as their King. The kings they would rather have will be false, but he is their true King. God is the true King.

Read these verses from the Psalms:

> Listen to my cry for help, my King and my God,
>   for to you I pray. (5:2)

The Lord is King for ever and ever. (10:16)

Who is he, this King of glory? The Lord Almighty –
   he is the King of glory. (24:10)

You are my King and my God. (44:4)

For God is the King of all the earth. (47:7)

I could go on, but I think the point is made. The true
King is God. So if Jesus is being shown to us by
Matthew as the opposite of the Herods of this world, as
more than a better king, but as God's true King, then
who are we being shown? God. We are being shown
that Jesus is God, the rightful and true King over all the
earth. No wonder this kingship theme is important to
Matthew. No wonder it gets linked to the worship idea.
No wonder that when Matthew has shown us the King,
he bids us worship at Jesus' feet. And so he rams this
home by taking us from the feeding of the five thousand into the next story in chapter 14 with the word
'immediately', and immediately we find ourselves in
another of the ten worship stories in the Gospel.

Wind, waves, walking and worship

After the feeding of the five thousand, Jesus sends the
disciples ahead of him across the lake in a boat. He stays
behind a while to pray, but the wind is against the boat
and although they make some headway, the disciples

have problems getting to the other side. So Jesus walks
across the water to help them. They see him and, terrified, cry out, 'It's a ghost.' He calms them, and Peter
asks Jesus to enable him to join him on the water.
'Come,' says Jesus. Peter does so, and walks on the
waves – till he looks down, sees what he is doing and
starts to sink in fear. Jesus gently rebukes him, and they
climb into the boat, where the rest worship Jesus and
declare him to be the Son of God (Matthew 14:22–36).

The first thing to notice is Matthew's use of contrasts
again: different reactions that make the same point;
different choices that highlight our choices. For there are
two confessions in this story: one of fear and one of faith.

When the disciples first see Jesus, they do not declare,
'It's the Lord,' or, 'You are the Son of God,' or even a
casual, 'Hello, Jesus. Taking a short cut?' 'They were
terrified,' says the text; they 'cried out in fear'. They
said, 'It's a ghost.' Now the truth is that if our worship
gives people sight of Jesus, gives them the experience of
encountering him, then this response is perfectly plausi-
ble, because for people who do not know Jesus or who
are not used to worship having that spiritual ring of
truth, a first encounter may be severely disorientating,
frightening. Something you don't think possible
happens, and fear is the result. But Jesus does not want
our fear. He speaks to the disciples: 'Take courage! It is I.
Don't be afraid.'

Then in the dialogue between Jesus and Peter, in his
care of Peter, in the gentleness of the rebuke and the
wonder of the action of walking on water, Jesus turns

their fear to worship. The disciples see the truth of Jesus' person and power, and the next time they speak it is a confession of faith: 'Truly you are the Son of God.' The result of the encounter is that for the first time since Jesus' public ministry began, the disciples are recorded as *worshipping* him; seeing his greatness, his greater-than-them-ness, coming towards to kiss the feet that walk on the waves, offering a true response of the people who know they have just seen God in action. And in their worship they recognise Jesus as King (this 'Son of God' title is a standard title for the Jewish king throughout the Psalms).

To worship Jesus is to recognise him for who he is, and to live in the light of that recognition. Not obeying God, fear of the elements around us, or even simple panic can sometimes simply be the result of failing to understand the nature and character of God. Matthew is intent upon his readers not making that mistake. Worship should change us as we recognise who Jesus is and what power he has to change us. Jesus is King and he has the power, he is in control, he is God. As we see Jesus more clearly through the lens of worship, obedience becomes easier. Understanding, fully understanding, that Jesus is King and that this means he has the character of the righteous God, the power of the almighty God and the desire to intervene for us as our loving heavenly Father, has to make a difference to those worshipping.

The impact on us of the idea that Jesus is our King ought to be huge. Many worshippers today come to a church service filled with fear or doubt or pain because for them the world and its problems seem too big to handle. Worshipping King Jesus should always remind us that he is greater – greater than the problems we face, greater than us, greater than the world. Robin Green puts it this way:

> There is a desire within people . . . to make sense of human experience. Liturgy, by providing a structure of meaning, helps us respond to that desire. It also creates a safe environment to push our questions hard and face perplexity. People come to church to be with God and to hide from God, to scream at God and to embrace God, to be with others and to be with themselves, to prepare for death and birth, marriage and divorce. Worship at its best is a place where people confront the depth of their own need in the presence of God.[4]

And this confronting is done because however big the problem, worship helps us see that God is bigger.

There is a song we used to sing a lot, which has the chorus, 'We will magnify the Lord enthroned in Zion.'[5] How can we magnify God? How can we make him bigger than he is? Well, obviously we cannot, but in our worship ('in Zion', in the imagery of the song) we allow God his proper perspective. We allow ourselves to step back and see things from God's angle. He is not objec-

---

4. Robin Green, *Only Connect*, p. 13.
5. Phil Lawson Johnston, 'We will magnify', Kingsway's Thankyou Music, Eastbourne, 1982.

tively bigger, but we realise more truly in worship his size and power, his authority over us and all things, and our worship has the effect of magnifying him in our lives. We let God be God. And as that happens, everything else gets put in its place. Our problems don't disappear, but we do see that God is bigger, so they become less fearful. Even the wind and the waves obey.

John Wimber commented on this while preaching through Romans. In chapter 4 of Romans we read of Abraham's faith in believing the promise of God that he would have a son, although both he and his wife Sarah were getting on a bit. Why did he believe? Wimber argues that the problem today is that people allow their problems to be bigger than their God, so they can't give up this habit or that bad practice. But Abraham shows what faith is: believing that God is bigger than any problem:

> On the one hand you have the promises of God, on the other you have 'reality' . . . it has not happened, but God said it would. How do you manage not wavering in your faith when everything in your scientific world-view says, 'No way! It's not happening!' . . . I've seen people do this with conversion – they come to Christ . . . then they fall back into their sin, then they repent and are restored, then they fall again, and by the time they've been through the cycle four or five times, they say, 'It's not working for me' . . . What's the problem? They believe their sin more than they believe their God. Instead of being like Abraham who looked at his body and his faith didn't waver, they looked at their sin life and their faith *did* waver . . . Many people

believe God, that is they believe about him, but they do not trust him with hard things.[6]

Our worldview is so focused on ourselves and our problems that sometimes we completely defeat our spiritual lives with the pessimism and hopelessness within us. Worship makes us look out from ourselves. Worshipping Jesus the King makes us look out with hope. For when life hits us with something we cannot master, worshipping Jesus the King shows us one who is Master of all things. Seeing him makes a difference.

The King who can

I was once at an informal praise gathering on a lovely summer's evening. The sun outside had that lustrous late-evening glow to it, and almost everybody attending the meeting was in shorts and T-shirt. It was a truly relaxed affair. The rector of that particular church was a lovely pastoral chap, with a congregation that included a few mad keen charismatics and also many who were more restrained in expressing their faith. He kept everybody together mostly by avoiding what he (and many of them) would have regarded as 'extremes'. On that evening, he welcomed us and I led the opening worship. We sang several songs, we prayed a while, and the sense of the presence of God was strong. Then one

---

6. John Wimber, 'Romans', cassette 4 of 16 from recorded sermon series (Vineyard Direct, 1999).

of those curious things happened that sometimes occur in church life: a lovely, godly woman in the congregation prayed for the Holy Spirit to come and fill each of us there. And it did not happen.

From that point, I felt the gathering became strained, with people almost competing to be the loudest singer, the most fervent pray-er. The rector seemed to struggle with his talk, and I have to admit I was actually glad when it was time to go home.

We all have ideas as to how worship should go. But if Jesus is not in charge, if he is not King, if we turn that order upside down and put ourselves in command, then all our good ideas remain just that – our good ideas. And to get this point across – that it is not just a matter of saying the right words at the right time, but a matter of really submitting in our hearts to King Jesus when we come to worship – Matthew tells the story about a Canaanite woman (Matthew 15:21–28).

The Canaanite woman has a daughter suffering terribly from demon possession. When she hears Jesus is in the area, she goes out to find him and, seeing him, cries out, 'Lord! Son of David! Have mercy on me!' And Jesus ignores her. He doesn't say a word. It gets so embarrassing that the disciples ask him to do something, because the woman keeps on shouting out at them. To the disciples Jesus simply says, 'I was sent only to the lost sheep of Israel.' This despite having healed a centurion's servant in chapter 8. 'She's not one of us, not a Jew; I'm not having anything to do with her' appears to be his attitude. It is Matthew 7:21–23 with a vengeance: 'Not everyone who says to me, "Lord, Lord," will enter the kingdom of heaven, but only he who does the will of my Father who is in heaven . . . I will tell them plainly, "I never knew you." '

But hold on a moment. Isn't this woman getting worship right? She calls Jesus 'Lord', and we have seen how important that is. She calls him 'Son of David', another title for God's King. What more can he want?

Quite a lot as it turns out. You see, I think that the charismatic lady of my story and this Canaanite woman were probably doing very similar things. I think they were – with the best will in the world – manipulating Jesus. Or trying to. The woman at the worship gathering was desperate for a real spiritual breakthrough and was working from super intentions, but she got it wrong. It was not her job that night to push people further than they could comfortably go. She was not the rector, she was not in charge, she could not see exactly what he was intending to achieve bit by bit in the life of that congregation. Or if she could see the goal, she just got impatient and wanted everything now! So by using the right words, she asked the Holy Spirit to come to her timing, her desire. Right words, but still manipulation. Still twisting God's arm. It wasn't a bad desire – just her own desire for something to 'happen' that night rather than God's desire.

The Canaanite woman is the same. 'Lord' is a good word to use when addressing Jesus. 'Son of David' rightly speaks of his kingship. Her daughter is in a terrible state, and the woman is right to seek Jesus. Except that Jesus is being used, exploited, taken advantage of, not worshipped.

Girls, if you want a bloke to do something for you, you know what to do: massage his machismo and make him feel good about himself. Pretend you can't open a jar of mayonnaise and ask a chap to do it for you. He'll feel so pleased at having demonstrated how strong he is and how good he is at rescuing damsels in distress that he'll do anything else you ask. You don't need the jar opening, but you do need him to feel good so you can ask for something else. You're just using the one thing to get to another. That's what the Canaanite woman is doing in the story: using words to flatter so that she can get what she wants. And Jesus does not even respond to her. Until, that is, she sees she is getting nowhere, and gets serious. The NIV tells us that 'the woman came and knelt before him', but in fact what she does is worship Jesus. The Greek says *prosekunei*, 'she worships'. What changes the story? The woman worships Jesus. She gets beyond the words, or rather she realises that words are not enough if they are simply used as tools to get what you want. You have to mean them. And she does mean them. She falls before Jesus, worships him, kisses his hand, making herself to be his servant, and in her worship she begs him to help.

Now he talks to her. Now we are being serious. But he does not make it easy. He pushes her into acknowledging that she is unworthy before him. It's a strange tale. Finally she says, 'Even the dogs eat the crumbs that fall from their masters' table,' again making Jesus greater than herself by calling him 'master'. And now her request is granted.

It seems we have travelled a long way to end this chapter pretty much where we began. Back in the story of the Magi and Herod we saw the contrast between those who come to worship Jesus in order to give, and those who come in order to get. Wise men who gave everything – their time, their careers, their families and their costly gifts; and a tyrant of a ruler who wanted to keep himself safe by taking an infant's life. And this Canaanite woman takes us through the same process: for sure she is coming to Jesus for the wrong reasons; she wants something from him. She wants her daughter back in her right mind, free from this demon that is tormenting her. And for as long as she's just using Jesus, he simply does not hear her. Her words are as silence, her pleas are mute, because her heart speaks only of herself. But when she breaks down, she breaks through. She simply worships Jesus, making him her focus, giving herself and her desires to him for him to handle as he will, and suddenly, giving everything to him, she is in a place where she can receive everything she dreamed of from him.

To give or to get? But it is in losing ourselves in worship that we find our King, and everything in our lives comes under his reign, his power, his authority. Worship is where Jesus rules as King, and where Jesus rules as King, his kingdom comes, his will is done and his people's prayers are answered.

God is no fool, but we are indeed foolish if we think

that we can use him to get what we want. He *will* grant us all sorts of things, often including those very things we think we really want, but not because we twist his arm, not because we say nice things about him and not because we butter him up. He pours out gifts on us because he is a giving God, and we put ourselves in a place to receive when we worship him as such. Really worship. And, says Matthew, that means making him King in our lives – letting him have first place, letting him have control – bowing before him in worship, acknowledging with our lips and our lives that he is greater, we are less. It's a humbling idea, but it is the heart of this *proskuneo* word: you are King and I will fall before you; you are King and I will serve you always; you are King and I will obey you in all things; you are King and I will sing your praise.

> Praise, my soul, the King of heaven;
> To His feet thy tribute bring.
> Ransomed, healed, restored, forgiven,
> Who like thee His praise should sing?
> Praise Him! Praise Him!
> Praise Him! Praise Him!
> Praise the everlasting King!
>
> *Henry F. Lyte*

6

More Than a Song

Say what you mean, and mean what you say. It's the kind of advice we would give to a child who had tried to deceive us by telling us that they fully understood a command not to steal ice-cream from the fridge – just before we caught them with chocolate chip all around their lips. 'If you are going to ignore me, then don't lie to me as well! And take that smirk off your face before I do it for you,' might be one loving parental response.

Of course sometimes there is the language barrier. We would love to say what we mean, but something gets in the way, some mental moment of madness, some malapropism that twists our meaning beyond our intentions.

I used to collect such *bon mots* when I was an undergraduate. I was the terror of the preachers in my church. I remember one guy (who had better remain nameless, though I must add I learned an enormous amount from him!) had a particular gift for the mixed metaphor. One Sunday evening, as he took us through a complicated passage of Scripture that needed us to hold on to several different ideas at the same time, he fearlessly commanded us to 'jot that down in your mind's eye'. I can't for the life of me remember what I was supposed to jot down in my mind's eye, because I spent so long wondering how I would do such a thing without injuring myself in the process!

Actually, all those preachers there got their own back on me the first time I was invited to lead prayers. I had everything carefully written out in front of me, because I knew that if I made the slightest blunder everybody would spot it and I would suffer for ages. Except, as I stood up to lead the prayers, I realised everybody else was standing as well and I needed to give them an instruction about posture before we began praying. So I looked up from my carefully prepared script and boldly invited them to 'please knit or seel to pray'.

Saying what you mean, and meaning what you say in worship is a major theme for Matthew's Gospel, and our focus for this chapter. If in our last chapter we saw how Matthew applies some of our theory on lordship to his first readers and hearers, now we are going to look at the way he applies our ideas of the Christian life as a life of worship. We said that worshipping God comes first and everything else follows. You make the worship choice, and that almost automatically makes the moral choice. To help us think about it we shall first look at two *proskuneo* worship stories that cover some of the ground for us; that make us think about the consequences of our choices – the way the things we choose in one area affect every area of our lives. Then in the light of those stories we shall look at two other areas of Jesus' teaching recorded by Matthew that are concerned with this issue.

Getting what you ask for

I once had the good fortune to ask Sandy Millar of Holy Trinity Brompton for some advice over a job I wanted to do. We were having lunch in a lovely Kensington bistro, and Sandy fixed his eye on me and said with that penetrating wisdom that underlies the genial, avuncular appearance most of us see most of the time, 'Sometimes, getting what you want is a form of judgement. Be careful what you ask for, Marcus. You might get it.'

He went on to talk about the passage from 1 Samuel 8 we looked at in the last chapter, where the people of Israel pestered the prophet Samuel to give them a king – a human king like the other nations around them had. Samuel was displeased, but prayed and asked God what to do. As we have seen, God's reply was that it was him they were rejecting, not Samuel. He was to tell them what a king would do, then give them one. So Samuel told the people that a king would subdue them, force them to serve him, rob them blind, take their daughters, lead them in needless war and make them his slaves.

But the people refused to listen to Samuel. 'No!' they said. 'We want a king over us. Then we shall be like all the other nations, with a king to lead us and to go out before us and fight our battles.' When Samuel heard all that the people said, he repeated it before the Lord. The Lord answered, 'Listen to them and give them a king.' (1 Samuel 8:19–22)

The people got what they asked for – and suffered all that they had been warned about. This was a judgement against them for rejecting God as their King. Without God as King they truly became just like the nations around them, as indeed they had wanted to be.

Well, in my youthful enthusiasm I ignored Sandy's advice and applied for the job. But God had mercy on me, and I didn't get it!

The story of Zebedee's wife in Matthew 20:20–28 is a story about being careful what you ask for; of saying what you mean and meaning what you say. Indeed, it is quite clear that on the most obvious level James' and John's mother had no idea what she was asking for, but Jesus answered her prayers anyway.

James' and John's mother comes to Jesus, worships him ('kneels before' in the NIV, but the Greek is *proskunousa*, literally 'worshipping'), and asks a favour: 'Grant that one of these two sons of mine may sit at your right and the other at your left in your kingdom.'

The setting is immediately before Jesus enters Jerusalem in triumph on the first Palm Sunday. The crowds are about to sing songs to him, welcoming him as Son of David; as the King coming in the name of the

Lord. And before it all happens, Zebedee's wife, seeing the new order that must surely come when God's King takes up his rule in Jerusalem, tries to get the best for her boys. If there will be a new government as the kingdom is restored to Israel, how about a taste of power for two faithful brothers? Not too much to ask, surely?

The problem is, the boys' mother has got everything wrong. She has failed to understand what this King will do when he enters Jerusalem. She thinks he will conquer Rome, but that is far too small an enemy for the man who within a week will conquer death. She thinks he will set up a new earthly order, when in fact Jesus is about to set up a new earth. She wants a ministry or two for her sons, power for the faithful. Ministry? Sure, says Jesus. Power? Let's think again.

Jesus contrasts wrong ideas about power with his own idea of power: 'The Son of Man did not come to be served, but to serve, and to give his life as a ransom for many.' We are not to do people down but to raise them up; not to make others less than us but to make them greater, and to give away ourselves in the process. The worship choice makes the moral choice: we worship this God, we get his standards. What is the power he gives away? The power he himself models: if you have power to lose yourself without fear, you have power. God's power is total, and totally to be used for the good of others, because that is the way God is.

Yet her worship was genuine. And she was prepared for the reality of her worship to affect her life and the lives of her family. Although her *understanding* both of

God's power and the events that were about to take place was out of line, her worship strangely still achieved its end. 'You will indeed drink from my cup,' said Jesus. And as the boys followed Jesus, they did drink from Jesus' cup – a cup of suffering and service and pain and perseverance. James endured an early martyrdom and John also suffered for his faith in Jesus.

Say what you mean. Our worship should show that when we pray with worshipping hearts, God hears and answers us. But his answers may surprise. If we are honest with God in worship, he will deal with us honestly. Worshipping God forbids hidden agendas – the secrets we keep from each other so that we can get ahead, win our day, get our way. Say what you mean.

This woman is truly worshipping. The difference between her and the Canaanite woman who came to Jesus with fine words but was just using him for her own ends is that this woman is giving everything she has to God. There is no request for mercy for her sons, no request that they should be kept safe and out of harm, no half-hearted following of the Lord. The worship choice is to put Jesus first; the moral choice (the life-of-worship choice, if you will) is to live without complaining about the consequences. They are going into Jerusalem, with its massive fortress and streets filled with Roman soldiers, and she gives her sons unreservedly to God: wherever Jesus goes, let one be on the right, one on the left. She is presuming victory, but she is putting her sons on the front line in the service of God. Do you think she ever regretted this little conversation? When

Jesus was crucified, do you think a shiver ran up her spine at the idea of her boys drinking the same cup? When James was put to death with the sword on Herod's orders, did she repent of her petition, a moment's madness, the enthusiasm of misplaced maternal love?

When I first spoke at home of the thoughts I was having of heading into full-time Christian ministry, my mother was not exactly thrilled. She wanted me to go to Oxford, become a lawyer, earn pots of money. So she tackled Tim, the chaplain at the hospital where she worked, hoping that he would roundly condemn my strange ideas and join her in dissuading me from such ill-conceived plans. Tim refused to do that, instead recommending that she pray that God's will would be done, and that whatever that might turn out to be, she would have the grace to accept it. Advice that has stayed with her, and now many years on she still quotes it at me as the ultimate in spiritual wisdom!

For a mother to wholeheartedly trust her children into God's keeping, whatever that might mean, whatever he might call them to do, wherever he might call them to go – for her to (as the saying goes) 'let go and let God' – is a sign of real worship.

Zebedee's wife worshipped God and dedicated her sons to his Son. She gave. She did not seek to gain anything for herself. She worshipped Jesus in full knowledge that this worship would change everything for ever. There is a totality to her worship that demands respect. When she worshipped Jesus, she meant what she said. Her heart for worship shines through all her confusion and lack of understanding, and gives us a model we ought to be pleased to copy. Matthew doesn't say that we have to get everything right when we worship. But when we give everything in worship, when we really mean it, then God will take us at our word and bless us.

Being true to your word

I read a list of popular lies recently – lies that are so commonplace, one could almost say they define certain aspects of our culture. Things like, when you call a company to make a complaint, the phone rings and then some soulless voice tells you, 'All our operators are busy' (and that might be the first lie), and that you are in a queue. You wait for ten minutes, listening to droning music, and then that voice comes back and says, 'We're sorry for the delay, but an operator will be with you shortly. Your call matters to us.' 'Sorry? Matters? Hah!' you feel like shouting down the line – if only there were somebody there to listen. Then when your call is taken, you are so afraid that if you sound too cross the line will cut out and you'll have to go through the whole thing again, that if the operator apologises for the delay, all you can say is, 'No problem. At least I'm through now.' No problem! We join in the lies!

The classic cultural lie of course is the simple line, 'Your cheque is in the post.' Or, slightly more subtly, in a society where films, TV and magazines all present casual sex as the norm, relationships as temporary and for selfish pleasures, and men as heartless brutes saying what they need to in order to get what they want, 'I love you too'. Ouch.

Maybe the word 'lie' is too strong. These are just social pleasantries, spoken to ease life along. They do not actually reflect any true emotion or event, but are said to make us feel better. They are the proverbs of the superficial society: words without content – all style and no substance.

It is a problem we face as worshippers. Given that we all indulge in these empty words from time to time as it's just the way our culture works, we need to guard against this way of thinking and speaking infecting our worship. Say what you mean, and mean what you say.

Matthew tackles this issue in a parable Jesus told about a master and two servants (18:21–35). Jesus tells this story in response to Peter asking a question about how many times one should forgive someone. A king is settling his accounts and calls in a slave who owes him a great deal but cannot pay. The king therefore orders him to be sold, as well as his family, in order to make good the debt. But the slave falls on his knees before the king (or, actually, as this is the Greek word *prosekunei* we should say he worships the king) and begs for mercy. He comes towards to kiss one who has power to condemn or forgive. The king has pity and cancels the debt. But this slave then imprisons a lesser slave who owes him much less, even though the lesser slave does beg for mercy on his knees. When the king is told of this, he calls the first slave back, and tells him that because he refused to show mercy on the other slave he will suffer after all. Jesus grimly finishes the tale with the comment, 'This is how my heavenly Father will treat each of you unless you forgive your brother from your heart.'

Worship changes things. Matthew gives us an example of how worshipping God brings salvation; of the things we looked at back in Chapter 4 of this book being worked out in the life of an individual. We said that sin was about worshipping the wrong things, the cross was about Jesus' perfect worship freeing us from the failure of wrong worship, and the Christian life was the result of right worship restored. We are made right with God by Jesus' complete worship of his Father on the cross, and now we walk in that right relationship, where we again worship God, and God alone, with all our hearts.

Isn't this what happens in the first part of the story? The servant has a debt to pay – a crushing, unbelievable debt that he could never pay. It affects every part of his life, and he stands to lose his wife, children, home, everything if he can't pay up. Just like us. Apart from Christ, the burden of sin is so great we could never give God what we owe him. Apart from Christ, the temptation to go after all the wrong things is so strong, we could never guarantee to love God alone. Judgement is pronounced, but as the servant in the parable hears the words, he falls in worship to the king, and promises to pay back the debt. He worships God and promises to go on worshipping God. And that worship changes everything. The judgement is lifted, the penalty removed, the punishment nowhere to be seen.

Worshipping Jesus is the opposite of sin. If we worship, we are getting life right because we are living out a right relationship with God: doing what we should be doing, being what we should be being, meaning what we say and moreover saying all the right things for once. Are you afraid you've missed the spiritual boat? Worship Jesus. Are you afraid your life is so bad God cannot love you? Worship Jesus. Are you convinced you can never be good enough? Worship Jesus. He will turn everything around as your whole world is turned the right way up simply by putting Jesus back at the top by worshipping him. Are you so sure of yourself that you think you've got life all sewn up? Worship Jesus. Are you pleased with the way you lead your life? Are you just a bit smug, and certainly grateful you are not the mess other people are? Worship Jesus. You might just be wrong, and putting Jesus first will bring you all the forgiveness you need too. It's for everyone, this forgiveness thing, and it comes free as we turn to Jesus and make him Lord, King, number one in our lives, by worshipping him.

However, God requires more than empty words. We have to mean what we say and sing. It really is more than a song; God really does look deeper than that. Worship is expressed in our words and songs, but it takes up our whole lives, and our whole lives bear the marks of change that worshipping God brings. And if there is no change, then Matthew is clear: there was no worship either, and that means you're still in trouble. The worship choice makes the moral choice. If the moral choice is absent or wrong, then the worship choice is in doubt too.

The servant, whose worship so impressed the king that he forgave him everything, goes out from the throne room and finds a chap who owes him a small amount of money. But when this guy can't pay, the first servant throws him in jail. Forgiveness has been received, but not given to anyone else. His worship changed the outcome of his life, in that he got out of jail, but not the character of his life, in that he refused to share with others the forgiveness that had been given to him.

They say that pets are like their owners, or that owners become like their pets. You spend long enough together and you pick up character traits, I guess. I must admit that both Matt, my Springer Spaniel, and I had our hair cut a fortnight ago. But he only needs it doing once or twice a year, and I still go a bit more frequently than that! I know someone, on the other hand, who used to have a big German dog, all muscle and sleekness to look at, but scatty as a goose, and I used to amuse myself by thinking how similar owner and pet were at times. For example, normally the owner in question is a good confident driver, but there are days when she gets all flustered, and at those times her resemblance to that dog is always naughtily near the front of my mind!

Well, we are not God's pets – we are his children and his friends – but we too are supposed to grow more like him. It's the relationship thing: we spend time with him, we learn what matters to him, and these cares and compassions of his become our cares and compassions. As we worship we are changed from one degree of glory to another, being made like him. 'The Spirit's work of transforming God's people is intrinsically related to the experience of worship.'[1] And if we are nothing like him, not caring for the things he cares for, having no compassion for those on whom he pours all his compassion, then questions have to be asked about our worship. Do we mean what we say? Or is it all just so many meaningless words?

We are being sold short if we are allowed for a moment to think that worship on Sunday is in any way divorced from the rest of life. Worship is all of life and it affects all of life, and the Sunday expression of our common worship must show this. Robin Gill puts it this way: 'Worship also makes strong demands upon us. It requires no less than we should go out into the world to love, to serve and to care.'[2] Or again: 'Loving God has everything to do with loving our neighbour, and loving our neighbour tells us much about whether and how we love God.'[3]

The implication from this parable Jesus taught is clear.

1. C. Cocksworth, *Holy Holy Holy*, p. 145.
2. R. Gill, *Moral Communities*, p. 23.
3. *Ibid.*, p. 13.

If we don't love our neighbour, if we don't forgive as we have been forgiven, then it seems our worship is empty and false. And such empty and false worship indicates a lack of relationship with a loving and forgiving God. And such a lack of relationship questions our whole Christian commitment. James says in his epistle, 'Faith by itself, if it is not accompanied by action, is dead' (James 2:17) and this is exactly the same point. Worship is not just songs and prayers; it is the life renewed and reformed by those songs and prayers. Jesus says very strongly in this story that if the life is not renewed and reformed then the songs and prayers that come with it are meaningless and will count for nothing before God. You've got to live it out, or you are not really alive at all.

Words are not enough

All churches have liturgy. Liturgy is simply the way we organise our worship. It may be the 1662 *Book of Common Prayer*, or it may be the charismatic six-songs-then-sermon-then-prayer-ministry, but we all do liturgy. And the way we organise worship – our liturgies, particularly lengthy written liturgies – can give the impression that if you know the words you have everything sorted. Now, good liturgy *is* good doctrine, but having the right words does not necessarily mean having a right heart.

After Pilate hands Jesus over to be crucified (Matthew 27:26–44), the story focuses on the curses poured out on Jesus by those around him. First the soldiers, then

passers-by, then the chief priests, teachers of the law
and elders, and finally the two thieves crucified with
him. But look at the words of their curses: 'Hail, king of
the Jews' (v. 29), 'This is Jesus, the King of the Jews' (v.
37), 'Come down from the cross if you are the Son of
God' (v. 40), 'He saved others' (v. 42), 'He's the King of
Israel' (v. 42), 'He trusts in God. Let God rescue him' (v.
43), 'The Son of God' (v. 43). These are all, it has to be
said, fairly good confessions of faith; that is, if you just
take the words. We would want words like these in all
our liturgies, affirming the kingship of Jesus, his status as
Son of God, his trust in God, his power to save. But
Matthew uses these words to draw one of his contrasts,
for quite obviously in the context of the day of Jesus'
death these were anything but affirmations of faith. The
words are true, but the hearts are not, so this 'worship'
has become mockery.

It is like the parable in Matthew 21:28–32, where
Jesus tells of a father with two sons. He asks both of
them to do a job and one says 'no'; the other 'yes'. But
the one who says 'yes' never gets round to doing the
job, while the other has a change of heart and gets the
job done. 'Which of the two did what his father
wanted?' asks Jesus. 'The first,' they reply. Worship that
is all the right words but comes from an empty heart
and has no effect on the life of the worshipper is meaningless. Worship that is flawed and incomplete yet
comes from a heart that wants to follow Jesus and a life
that lives out that choice receives the Master's approval.
Just like Zebedee's wife.

And aren't the priests supposed to be the ones who worship the true God? Yet they join the soldiers' mockery of Jesus. When Jesus dies, and the temple curtain is torn, and some of the dead around the city are raised there and then to life, however, it is not the priests but the soldiers whose mockery turns full circle: 'Surely he was the Son of God!' they cry (Matthew 27:54). And truth genuinely finds itself on the lips of sinners whose hard hearts have been changed.

We are left in no doubt by Matthew that these soldiers made the right choice, and that although they were foreigners and oppressors, their choice should be our choice. By contrast, nowhere do the priests take back their words of Matthew 26:65, where on hearing Jesus himself confess that he is the Son of God, the Christ, they declare baldly, 'He has spoken blasphemy!' The leaders of God's people are not immune from getting these choices wrong, and some of Matthew's harshest words are reserved for these leaders whose words were the most impressive, seemingly the holiest, certainly the strictest and supposedly the most biblical.

Woe, woe and thrice woe?

Matthew devotes a whole chapter (23:1 – 24:2) to a tale of seven woes to the Pharisees for their abuse of worship and what it does to people; of how words without truth destroy the soul; of how bad lives point out the emptiness of hollow words of worship. This is one of those passages that any preacher recognises as a sermon outline: it has an introduction, a main section (here of seven separate points, not three!) and a conclusion. Jesus' teaching on the subject is thorough and thought through. Yet even as he denounces bad practice, all is not 'woe, woe and thrice woe'. Almost every step carries alternatives, where Matthew sets before us good and bad options so that the right way forward is constantly offered.

The introduction (Matthew 23:1–12) makes two opening points about the shortcomings of the Pharisees: they talk a good fight, but they don't land any punches (vv. 2–4), or, as Jesus puts it, 'They do not practise what they preach.' Their words are empty, they have no integrity. And secondly, they seek recognition and honour for themselves rather than God – their religion is self-centred; empty and selfish; all about me. Hardly a glowing character reference for the men who saw themselves as being responsible for regulating most Jews' understanding of regular public worship. We too know these dangers: on the one hand failing to live up to God's standards, letting ourselves and those around us down by careless words or deeds when stressed or angry, or just getting it wrong, and on the other hand succumbing to the temptation to do something that will make our friends say how good we are (though they never quite realise just how good that is), which will feed our ego and give us the place we deserve in the church or community. Common temptations. Common failings.

You know what I mean. It's been one of those days

where everything has gone wrong, and you are in a foul mood. The final straw comes when a girl you fancy walks past you without a glance, and all the horror of the day comes out of your mouth with a casual muttered curse. But the girl hears. She turns and sees you now, and she says those immortal words, 'Call yourself a Christian?'

Or, on the other hand, watching *Pop Idol* with a group of mates, you laughed with the rest of them as one of the contestants was told off for 'fishing for compliments'. At least, you laughed till one of the lads turned and said, 'That's just like you.' And he was right.

The point is that we all have these failings to some degree. They are common problems.

And they have common answers: we must practise what we preach, and if the standards we lay on people are tough, we have to help them live them out and demonstrate godliness by our own lives. We must be gentle with those who need correction, and remember God's economy: 'Whoever exalts himself will be humbled, and whoever humbles himself will be exalted.' So I must dare to trust that as a leader I can let go of my ego. I have a God who will do me all the good I can take if I put him first and not me. I must trust that simply worshipping him will change me over time, making me to be the servant of God that in my heart I long to become. It's the fulfilment of the dog owner's prayer: 'Lord, make me the man my dog thinks I am!' It may not win me prizes here and now, but one day I will see the smile on the face of the Lord of glory and hear

the words, 'Well done, good and faithful servant.' The
words I speak must have meaning, must be lived out in
the life of worship.

The rest of Matthew 23 goes on to give us hard
choices that serious worshippers must face. We all know
we should practise what we preach; that saving face can
stop us from doing what is right; that we have customs
and rules we believe in and don't keep (but insist others
do); that we lose sight of our priorities; that we get
hooked up on the little things that make us forget the
big picture; that sometimes it is plain easier to hide a
sinful heart with a smiling face than to sort out the sinful
heart, though we know we should deal with it. We all
know these things. Matthew makes us look straight at
them. He gives us no easy road out. Bad worship
choices lead to death. That's his simple message. Good
choices lead to life. Which do we want?

Making life choices, ordinary decisions in the ordinary
world, is no easier than this. But making those right
worship choices achieves two distinct goals. First, facing
hard choices in worship and learning to get them right
trains us for the rest of life beyond the worship hour.
Secondly, as I argued earlier, making the right worship
choice and living out the implications of those choices
makes many of these right moral choices for us.
Worship shapes life; it is not an escape, an extra, an
added bonus for those who are musical or artistic or
culturally middle-class. It is essential for every person to
choose to worship God, because only from making that
choice can any person begin to live a godly life, which is

the truth of our communal worship walked out day by day.

A way forward

When I was a child I used to have this recurring nightmare. It would always happen when I had the flu, and the fever was rising to its peak. One of my tasks in our house was peeling the potatoes for supper, and in the nightmare there were 954 potatoes to peel. As I looked at the mountain of spuds before me, I despaired of ever finishing this impossible task.

As we come to the end of this chapter on saying what we mean and meaning what we say in worship – on facing the realities of some of the implications for life that our worship should make us face – you may be feeling elated or deflated: excited at the scope of worship and the way it affects our lives, or slightly depressed at the truths you have read and how little your life bears the marks of the worshipping heart.

Linette Martin, in her wonderful book *Practical Praying*,[4] sums up how we can feel when we are challenged by God to go beyond where we are comfortable, and it is not easy. She is talking of 'prayer-language', but it applies to what we say in worship too.

---

4. Linette Martin, *Practical Praying* (Eerdmans, 1998) – my favourite book on prayer.

It is possible to use prayer-language to avoid God. When he comes too close – quick! throw some words into his face: something emotional by us or something beautiful by Cranmer. Maybe God will be satisfied and leave us alone. I am sometimes discouraged at how quickly I can react to the sound of his approaching feet. The gentlest drawing near on his part and I slam the door, 'No, no! I came to prayer (or to church) to feel comfortable and comforted. Not this! My only petition is: Go away!'

But remember, because of Jesus, we can get this right! Yet physically we find ourselves still living in this old world of sin, and that keeps on dragging us back. It's the now and the not yet – the kingdom breaking in, but not here in all its fullness. We have to remember this, and we have to remember that Christ who died for us that we might worship God with all our hearts has not abandoned us, even if we've just slipped up. His love is not a skittish goose that can be scared off by a moment's sin crying 'boo'. J. B. Torrance put it this way: 'Grace means that God gives himself to us as God, freely and unconditionally, to be worshipped and adored. But grace also means that God comes to us in Jesus Christ as man, to do for us and in us what we cannot do.'[5]

Worshipping God is at the core of how we work out our Christian lives. But it is also the gift of God to us in Christ Jesus, the cause and the purpose of our salvation. Its standards are high, but, to paraphrase Deuteronomy

---

5. J. B. Torrance, *Worship, Community and the Triune God* (Paternoster Press, 1996), pp. 54–55.

30, not so high we can't reach them, not so far from us we must give up, not so impossible only the spiritual super-heroes can attain them. By the grace of God, what we long for is in our hearts and on our lips already.

Back to basics

Jesus raises the stakes in Matthew 5:48, where he commands his hearers to 'be perfect, therefore, as your heavenly Father is perfect'. Do the standards now seem too high? But he goes on straight away to address the small things, the basic things, the simple things of our Christian lives. Worship comes first; it is the priority, the *sine qua non*. You make the worship choice first and that will affect the whole of the rest of your life. My grandmother understood this principle. She would often say to me, 'You look after the pennies, and the pounds will look after themselves.' Quite so. Jesus tells his followers to do the basics – to tend the relationship with God – and watch what happens.

Worship involves the whole of life, the whole of the way we live out the implications of our words and songs. But the focus is not the implications. The focus is still the relationship with Jesus, worshipping him day by day.

What does Jesus say in Matthew 6? Remember the basics. In the way you work out your worship, sure, give to the needy, but don't worry about people knowing what you are doing. Do it quietly, between you and God. Pray too, but not for the benefit of others' ears. Do it between you and God. Just say what you mean and mean what you say. Pray by yourself, pray always, for prayer is the language of worship. As you pray, the things you receive become the things you give to others. Forgive as you have been forgiven – that's a sure sign your worship of God is changing you. Fast too, but secretly. It is between you and God. All your promises and all your worship are to God. If you mean what you say, your life will bear it out. Your heart will be with God, and he will be your Master, your Lord, your King. Look to God, worship him, live in a right relationship with him day by day, and the life will follow. Don't be afraid, don't be discouraged, don't be overwhelmed by the implications of your worship of God, huge as those implications are. Keep your eyes fixed on the Saviour and he'll show you. As Jesus said, 'Seek first his kingdom and his righteousness, and all these things will be given to you as well' (Matthew 6:33).

And I have the distinct impression that when he said it, he meant it.

7

Tell Me the Stories of Jesus

Well, I don't know about you, but after that last chapter I need a bit of a change of pace. So let's take our ease, make sure we are sitting comfortably, and enjoy a few stories. Worship stories. Stories of how Jesus changed people's lives as they worshipped him. Some of these stories are from Matthew's Gospel; some have been written specially for us by friends of mine, reflecting some of the ideas of the Gospel in their own experience. One is my own story.

The Leper's Tale (Matthew 8:1–4)

Jesus has just finished preaching the Sermon on the Mount. It's been a long and challenging talk, pulling no punches, surprising his listeners both with his demands on their lifestyles, and with his authority. Jesus' teaching lacked words like 'perhaps', 'maybe', 'on the one hand' or 'I think'. His ending was particularly striking, where he told his hearers not just to listen to his words but to put them into practice. Listening by itself was no mark of godliness. Doing had to be there too.

So, true to his own words, as soon as he finishes speaking, he does some 'doing' himself. The crowds follow him down the mountainside, and at the bottom there is a leper. The crowds falter a little, wanting to be near Jesus, but not wanting to be anywhere near this sick man. The leper ignores them. They are not why he is here. He really is unaware of their presence – indeed, normally he does keep far away from other people. He has to by law. But he sees Jesus and he sees hope. He kneels at Jesus' feet and worships him.[1] He knows that this man is greater than he is; that this man is greater than all; that this man is worth worshipping. This man Jesus can make a difference, so he worships him – his frail, crumbling flesh comes towards to kiss perfection. The crowd is surprised. They are not just hanging back now; they are keeping quiet. A silence descends – they want to hear what the teacher will say. I mean, the man's sermon was cool, but *worshipping* him is going a bit far. Perhaps Jesus will rebuke the leper.

But it is the leper who speaks first: 'Lord, if you are willing, you can make me clean.'

His words cut through the silence like scissors through silk, allowing no one the chance to shake the teacher's hand and thank him for his lovely sermon. The

---

1. Verse 2: *prosekunei* – 'he worships'.

surface has been broken, this man has plunged deeper, and everyone else is caught up in the ride. A new spell has been cast, a new silence develops, a new anticipation rises. This leper actually believes Jesus has the power to heal his leprosy; to cure the incurable. He worships Jesus as if he were God, and adds to his act of worship words of worship: you can do the impossible, you can heal me. Lord. Almighty One, Loving One, the one who intervenes for me.

Then Jesus reaches out his hand and touches him. The entire crowd catch their breath as one – they can't help themselves. It's a real comedy moment, actually: unrehearsed but flawlessly choreographed. Except no one laughs. You just don't touch lepers. It's against the law. It makes you unclean, and it probably gives you the disease too. Jesus should have ignored the man. Or smiled sadly and walked on. He should have reminded him that God alone does these things. He should have quietly had his entourage push the leper to the back, out of sight and out of mind. No one would have objected. Everyone loved the talk and no one wanted to see the teacher embarrassed.

But Jesus' eyes are fixed on the man before him. The leper does not see the crowd, and suddenly neither does Jesus. 'If I'm willing? Of course I'm willing,' he smiles at the leper. And then he turns the world upside down. You see the way the world works is like this: everybody wants to be pure and holy, but purity and holiness are hard work and fragile. You get there for a moment, but something dirty comes along and sullies your hands or your mind, and you lose it again. So you have to be careful. It's like a white sheet. No sooner have you washed it than along comes the dog, paws dripping with mud, and jumps up as you're folding the nice clean sheet, and there are paw prints everywhere. Even if you try to hide the dirt, you know it's there, and it spreads. So if you touch someone who is unclean, you become unclean. Unclean wins, every time.

Not this time. 'Be clean,' says Jesus. And the leprosy fades away. White skin turns pink. Peeling, fraying, crumbling flesh becomes whole. Like new. Clean wins. Clean beats unclean. Clean transfers itself to unclean, and the marks of purity cover the stains of impurity, and the way the world works is turned on its head. It's as if two people in a room, one of them suffering from the flu, the other fearing to breathe in in case she gets it too, have decided that actually they want to change roles. And the sick one breathes in and catches good health off the other.

This is what worshipping does to us. It brings us face to face with Jesus. And we see that he's not just a teacher; he's the Lord – the all-powerful, loving Lord who intervenes for us and changes our lives. He is the King who brings his kingdom to us. A kingdom where healing conquers sickness and life conquers death. And yes, we live in a rotten old world where we don't see the fullness of God's rule, and sometimes it seems the old way still wins, but worship opens our eyes, our hearts, our lives to the possibility of King Jesus reigning.

And you can add all the ifs and buts you like – all

those things Jesus forgot to say in the sermon that he preached just before this event – but the Bible is clear. The leper worshipped Jesus. Jesus healed the leper. What are we supposed to understand? That healing happens when we worship. Physical healing? Yes. Inner healing? Sure. Mental and emotional healing? You bet. Why? Because when we worship Jesus we enter into the salvation order – the way God means life to be. Sin is worshipping the wrong things. Jesus died on a cross to open up for us the way to getting worship right; a path to right relationship with the Father in the power of the Spirit, and when we worship him we walk that path and see that power. Not completely, because that is reserved for the new heaven and the new earth and the glory of the age to come, but it starts now. Or else why did Jesus teach us to pray for his kingdom to come on earth as in heaven? Why ask for daily bread today, if we have to wait till that great and glorious day before our prayers will begin to be answered?

It's like the film *Pleasantville*, where a teenage brother and sister find themselves in a world designed like a 1950s sit-com. It is pleasant, bland and literally black and white, for the majority of the film is shot in black and white. However, as people discover emotions, passions, deeper things, bursts of colour start to appear. It is a film with many magical images: a black-and-white street with a red rose; a row of monochrome shops and a startling colour mural at the side of them; grey faces turn pink. Just as colour bursts piece by piece, item by item, into the picture in that film, so the kingdom of

God bursts into our world of grey and sin and sickness as we worship our Lord Jesus. Piece by piece. Bit by bit. Person by person.

A leper worships Jesus and catches good health.

The Daughter's Tale (Matthew 9:18–26)

There is a ruler. Mark tells us in his Gospel that he was a ruler of the synagogue and his name was Jairus. Matthew does not name him or tell us about the synagogue. He is just a ruler and a grieving father. It is a sad world where parents outlive their offspring, seeing their hopes for the future – that their children would have a better life than they – dashed prematurely. She was a child. Now she is just a frail, tiny body in a shroud. He will not see her married. He will not see her children. He will not see her again.

But one of the godfearers in town, a centurion who has been a sympathiser towards the religion of the Jews for many years, and more recently an exceptionally devout man, comes to see the synagogue ruler. They know each other well. When the synagogue was in need of repair, the centurion approached Jairus and offered to rebuild the whole thing, and Jairus accepted.[2] Although a Roman soldier could never be fully converted to Judaism (most regiments had their own

2. A slight reading into the material, but compare Matthew 8:5–13 with Luke 7:1–10. It is not far-fetched to imagine a synagogue ruler hearing from the man who rebuilt the synagogue, is it?

religious ceremonies and allegiances, though they didn't all have to worship the Emperor; that was a later development) he could become a godfearer: a Gentile who came to worship the God of the Jews from afar, not having all the benefits of being a member of God's chosen people, but being allowed to join in much of their worship and community life.

This centurion has a story to tell. His servant had recently been suffering from the most debilitating illness – he had been paralysed, and the centurion had feared for his life. Then the teacher from Nazareth, Jesus, about whom everybody was talking, came to Capernaum and the centurion had gone to him, asking for help. Jesus had not even gone into the man's house. He just heard the request, blessed him and told him the servant was well – and he was right. When he got home, he found his servant sitting up, recovering, and the change came at precisely the time he had been talking to Jesus.

Now, a death might be different. But if he could reverse such a dangerous illness without even being present, perhaps it might be worth seeking out this Jesus and asking for his help?

Jairus misses his daughter and wants her back. Part of him knows the situation is hopeless, but another part of him experiences that strange rebirth of hope that can be so powerful in the soul of someone who has been living in despair. He grabs his cloak and goes to find Jesus. As he goes, with every step the hope grows stronger. He knows the stories; he's seen the leper who has started coming to the synagogue because Jesus has healed him; he knows his centurion friend is a devout but sensible man. Surely these people were right. Surely Jesus would raise his daughter. Surely this man who had no fear of sickness would not be afraid of death.

In the market-place, Jesus is surrounded by a group of John's disciples – desert men, very frugal in their lifestyle; it is unusual to see them in the town itself. Jairus waits on the edge of their conversation, inwardly urging them to finish their talk of whether they should fast or feast. Eventually he can bear it no longer. He just throws himself down before Jesus and worships him.[3] A synagogue ruler worshipping another man – a shocking sight. But it all comes tumbling out of the poor man's heart. In his grief he sees more clearly than he has ever seen anything in his entire life: this Jesus is greater than he. He is in some special way from God, and worship is the only appropriate response. He bows and worships. Afraid of death he kisses the Lord of life and pours out his heart to him. 'My daughter, my dear sweet daughter, my pride and joy, my only daughter – she has, God have mercy, she has died. Jesus, my daughter is dead. But you can help. You can do anything. Just put your hand on her – this hand that has healed so many – and she will live.'

Jesus stands up and accompanies Jairus back to the house. Just as with the leper, the ruler receives no criticism for this act of worship. Jesus takes it and responds to it.

---

3. Matthew 9:18: *prosekunei* – 'he worships'.

On the way to the house, a woman who has suffered from a flow of blood for the last twelve years sees Jesus in the midst of the procession with his disciples and Jairus. They look purposeful. Clearly they have somewhere to go, something to do. This is her chance. No one will notice her on a day like this. She's a woman and she's ceremonially unclean, so she could never go to see Jesus as Jairus has just done, but she too wants help. Maybe if she just brushed past him in the press of the crowd it would be enough for her healing? All the doctors have failed. All her money has gone. But here at last is one final hope.

But, how embarrassing, when she touches his cloak he stops the procession. All those men. All those eager religious young men. All looking at her. Everybody turns and stares. Then she hears Jesus' voice: 'Take heart, daughter.' And she lifts her eyes from her feet and meets his gaze. 'Your faith has healed you.' And she knows it is true. She feels it. She stands stock still, puts her hand to her stomach, and tears fill her eyes as she realises that at last the pain, the shame, the misery, is all over. When she clears her eyes and looks up again, she is alone. They have gone. She rushes after them, wiping her eyes and her nose, laughing. Actually laughing. How long has it been since that happened?

Back at Jairus's house Jesus sees the wailing mourners and flute players playing on the family's grief. It is a part of Jewish life. Death is surrounded by noise. Sorrow is worn loudly, sadness demonstrated to all. Everybody joins in, including the neighbours and hangers-on. It would be disrespectful not to. But Jesus calls for silence. 'Go away,' he commands. 'There's no death here. The girl's asleep.' And the mourners laugh, but not as the woman who has just been healed laughed, for there is no joy in this sound. Only derision. Jesus speaks to Jairus, and he empties the house. His hope has grown fragile again at the sight of all the mourners, the reality of the girl's death hitting him hard. But Jesus is here, and he obeys the teacher. The mourners are put out, in more ways than one – and Jesus comes in.

'Little girl, get up,' he says gently, but with authority that makes Jairus look away from the tiny shroud and stare at Jesus himself. And he sees Jesus reach out his hand, and his hand is met by a smaller hand, coming from the shroud. Jairus follows this hand to its arm and its body and sees his daughter – his dear, dead daughter – and she gets up. Alive.

Now this story tells us three things that happen when we worship. The first is like the story of the leper, but carried to the ultimate degree. The wholeness of God conquers sickness as the leper worships Jesus. The kingdom of God is made present as he worships, and the effect of the coming kingdom is that he is physically healed. Here, life conquers death. Death is a result of the Fall. If there had never been any sin, there would never have been any death. The sinless Jesus, the obedient Jesus, simply works out the result of true worship to its ultimate degree. No sickness, no death. For now, what happens to this girl is just a sign of these things because she will die again. But Jesus' own death on the cross is followed by true resurrection. Perfect worship destroys sin and all its works. Death is swallowed up in victory.

The second lesson of the story is the role of hope in worship. Worship is both a sign and a cause of hope. Worship causes hope because as we worship the God who never changes, as we read and sing of his character, his power and his desire to intervene in our lives, we remind ourselves of what our God is like, and the reminder of truth works its power over the temptation to despair. It is like Asaph in Psalm 77, where he feels rejected by God, forgotten, left behind. Then it occurs to him to remember what God has done; to praise him for his works in times gone by; to recall God's holiness, God's power, God's involvement with his people. And hope returns. Robin Green describes this process as looking to the past so we can dare to face the future, letting our common worship show us that as God has worked for others he will work for us:

> Liturgy puts us in touch with the memory of who we are and our given-ness in order to adapt to the future given by Christ. It enables us to feel part of a history in which others have identified the same fundamental questions and discharged the same screams of terror against existence. Through it we also discover that today is not the end of the world.[4]

Everyone panics. Everyone doubts. Everyone despairs.

---

4. Robin Green, *Only Connect*, pp. 16–17.

Worship should remind us of this, and of how Christians get through these panics, doubts and despairs by seeing the God who is greater and unchanging. Jairus must have known the centurion's story. But he worships Jesus not as someone who is Lord for someone else, but as his own Lord. We hear the stories of faith, and worship makes us make that same leap. We do not worship Jairus's Lord; we worship Jesus as our own Lord. In our own time. Over our own lives.

> We all need to tell our own story in order to make sense of it, to make the links between past and present so both may connect with the future . . . But Christian liturgy also tells the story in a very particular way. It goes on retelling the story of Jesus because through that story we are to make sense of our own stories.[5]

Worship is the sign of hope because it takes us from the absorption of self and makes us look beyond our own experience to the objective truth about God.

Thirdly, worship alters our sense of the importance of time. What I mean is that we want instant solutions. The leper got an instant solution and I want one too. Spud, a friend of mine, puts it this way: 'What do we want? Patience. When do we want it? Now!' Buy now, pay later. Six months' interest free credit. The whole world wants everything now, and we are swept along. But please note that Jairus had to wait. He had to wait until

---

5. *Ibid.*, p. 17.

Jesus got to his house. The centurion did not have to wait. Jesus said, 'Now!' and now it was. But sometimes that is not so. Moreover, the woman with the haemorrhage delayed them on their way to Jairus's house, and that is a fascinating thing. Jesus had time for her, because he knew it would not affect what he was about to do for Jairus. We just do not work that way. We hear a promise or a calling from God, and we want it fulfilled now. If it isn't immediate, we presume we heard wrong.

I first heard the Lord call me to ordained ministry when I was 16 years old. Actually, it all came about because I was the reverse of normal teenage Christianity – a Christian at school, but not at home. I was a Christian for maybe three or four years before admitting it at home. I went to the school Christian Union, but not to church, because I expected to be made fun of at home. But then the school CU planned a Christmas houseparty and I really wanted to go. It was being held at a lovely place, Heightside, which was then run by the European Christian Mission, and is now where one of the Neville brothers of Manchester United lives. So I asked my dad if I could go. He looked at me, surprised, and asked, 'Are you a Christian then?' And I (rather Peter-like) replied that I was interested. There was no harm in being interested. But my sister reported this to my mum, and then Mum and I had a blazing row. Mum knew what Catholics were. She knew what Protestants were. But she had never heard of 'Christian Union' and presumed that they were Mormons or Jehovah's Witnesses and that I had been brainwashed. At the peak of our argument she screamed at me, 'You're not going to be a vicar, are you?'

Well, as I said, I did not even go to a church at that time. But something deep inside me said 'yes' and I never doubted it. So I said 'no', but I knew different. I was ordained eleven years later. Eleven years is quite a while. At times, I have to confess, I wondered if I had heard right. It is an odd way to receive a call. But when God has spoken, he has spoken, and he will do it. Our worship needs to capture this faithfulness of God. For me, that is one of the reasons I think corporate worship should be filled with Scripture. It is easy to doubt God until you are surrounded by the Scriptures, which cry out on every page that God is faithful; that he fulfils his promises; that he never lets us down even when we so often fail him. Jairus did not get an immediate answer. He had to wait. But he had worshipped Jesus and he knew that Jesus would not disappoint.

This is the God we meet as Jairus worships Jesus: the Lord of time, the Lord of hope and the Lord over life and death.

Things I would ask him to tell me . . .

Now, all the way through this book we have thought of worship as being the entire Godward response of our lives focused in corporate expression; that is to say, worship is the way we lead our lives in thanksgiving to God. But it needs to be expressed when we are church together. What follows is a collection of stories written by people today of their experiences of worship, and how it has changed them. All of them have picked moments of corporate worship as the focus for their stories, but each of these moments then goes on to affect how they live their lives. The point of all this is simple: Matthew gives us such stories so we can learn from them; I am giving these in order to emphasise his stories, and to show that the biblical principles we learn in Matthew's Gospel really do run true in our world today.

The Youth Chaplain's Story

Paul Thompson is an Anglican clergyman in South Wales. After several years in pastoral ministry he worked as a full-time youth chaplain in the Diocese of Llandaff, before returning to parish ministry in Lisvane, Cardiff. This is his story.

This is really a conversion story, although I suppose it is also a story of the Prodigal returning. I had been brought up in a Christian home and had 'given my heart to the Lord' when I was eight years old. We were in the Salvation Army and I was involved in all the Army things. I was in the Corps Cadets (Bible study), Singing Company (choir), Band, Sunday school, etc. It was assumed that I would go into full-time ministry as an officer, so I became a candidate for officership. Then I went to university and dropped God like a stone!

My life became a student's life – lots of parties, occasion- ally drinking too much, with some study mixed in. A

Salvation Army friend was concerned about me and asked if I would read the Gospels again as a favour to her. I liked her so I promised I would! I read the Gospels and really nothing clicked at all until I read John 6. As Jesus developed his argument I was more and more confused about this whole 'bread of life' stuff, then I read verse 53 and stopped reading: 'I tell you the truth, unless you eat the flesh of the Son of Man and drink his blood, you have no life in you. Whoever eats my flesh and drinks my blood has eternal life, and I will raise him up at the last day.'

I promised there and then that I would go to church the very next Sunday (25 January 1976). It was the Conversion of St Paul. Coming from the Army, I knew nothing of church calendars, ritual, sacraments, etc. I was really impressed therefore by the coincidence of my first time in church being the celebration of the conversion of my namesake! The service was Communion, which was cele-brated in a traditional 'high church' style, none of which made any sense to me at all, yet I knew that what was happening made a connection with what I had read in John 6. The references in the service to bread and wine, and the ceremonies and rituals that gave significance to these references, seemed to me to talk the same language as John 6. As everyone went forward for communion, and I was left alone in the pew, I knelt down and simply said to the Lord that I had no idea what all this was about, but that I was willing to take whatever next step he asked of me. Five months later I was baptised and confirmed, and 15 months after that I was at theological college preparing for the priesthood!

Now this story fits into a kind of experience that many

people understand: coming from a Christian family, moving away from the restraints that imposes, and then returning to God as an adult. Sometimes, although the moving away process scares the parents silly, it seems as though it is necessary for the child to develop their own faith separately from the family tradition in order for that faith to have real lasting strength.

In Paul's case there are three things that made a difference: a friend, reading the Gospels and attending a service of worship. The friend asked him to read the Gospels as a personal favour, and because he liked her, he did it. He read through three and a bit Gospels before anything hit home. To keep on reading that far without any sense of meaning coming through the pages shows that Paul must have liked this girl a lot, or he had some feelings (possibly of guilt) about his Army past that kept him going, or actually the Lord was drawing him on, even though he didn't understand it at the time. It was probably a mixture of all these things.

But when he hit a passage that intrigued him (and remember, the Salvation Army do not celebrate the sacraments, so communion had never been a part of this student's life), his response was to go to a service of worship. He did not understand; he was intrigued. But in order to get further on with God, a God he had been running away from, he decided to worship. Good choice. The leper in Matthew 8 has a problem. How does he overcome it? He goes to worship Jesus and to ask him to do something. The Canaanite woman in Matthew 15 has a problem. She goes to Jesus, but it is not until she worships him that everything changes. So Paul, faced with an issue he didn't understand, decided the only thing to do was worship. He went to church.

When he got there, did he suddenly understand everything in a blaze of existential glory? No. Was the experience of worship so powerful it pushed him to the floor with the weight of the presence of a God he could no longer deny? No. So what happened? 'As everyone went forward for communion, and I was left alone in the pew, I knelt down and simply said to the Lord that I had no idea what all this was about, but that I was willing to take whatever next step he asked of me.'

This is worship. Putting my life in God's hands – like the leper, like Jairus, like the Canaanite woman, like the mother of James and John. Letting him have control. Making him number one. Making him Lord. And how do we know this is true worship, and not just a moment's religious enthusiasm? Because it changed Paul's life. Baptised, confirmed and in theological college within two years of this experience, he had said he would do whatever God asked of him, and he did it.

When I see Paul leading people in worship, I see a man who means what he says, who backs up his words with his actions, and I see a man who may lead others because he walks out a life of worship himself.

The Archbishop's Story

Rowan Williams is Archbishop of Canterbury and head of the worldwide Anglican Communion. He is also a godly man I admire enormously, and was the bishop who ordained me as an Anglican priest. This is his story.

I think that one of the first occasions when I really became overwhelmingly conscious of God's reality was the first time I attended an Orthodox Liturgy – as a schoolboy of about 15. I don't think that I had ever before sensed that *being carried along* in worship that so many associate with Eastern Christian worship. What mattered was not my ideas or feelings as such: the process just unfolded with a kind of steady fullness, very like being caught up in a choral performance of a certain kind. It didn't 'wait' for you to get hold of it. So the effect was of being gently eased away from your own preoccupation, and so made aware of a twofold otherness – the great swell of worship all around, creation praising God, and ultimately the Son praising the Father; and the mysterious reality beyond or ahead, drawing that praise out. When I started thinking seriously, years later, about the movement at the heart of the Trinity, it was this experience that helped direct me. But my memory of what happened at the time was of the sheer force of being held and moved – and, the evening after the liturgy, finding my personal evening prayer quite transformed by all of this.

Whenever in later years worship has deeply worked upon me, this has always been the experience underlying it. I recognised something of the same (although it will sound strange, perhaps) at work in the revival and renewal services I attended in a local Baptist chapel later in my teens; in the monastic services I went to as a theological student at Mirfield; more recently in renewal events locally, especially one occasion a few years ago in a small valley church – a deep underlying silence leading into a sort of helplessness before God. When Archbishop Anthony Bloom described prayer as becoming vulnerable to God, I thought I knew a little of what he must mean because of these experiences.

Now this story is similar to Paul's, but different. Paul felt himself called *back* to God as he worshipped; Rowan felt himself called *into* God. It was an almost mystical experience: reality shifted for a while, and greater realities forced themselves into his consciousness. He was not alone in worshipping God – it was not just that group in that place – it was the worship of all creation that he could sense around him. The immensity of that feeling produced a humbling silence before Almighty God. Rowan was drawn out of himself and, as it were, placed before the throne of heaven, vulnerable, worshipping as he had never worshipped before. The worship gave a vision of God, an understanding of God. That vision and understanding has shaped an important part of Rowan's life and ministry.

I wonder if this was the experience of the wise men. What happened when they worshipped the infant Jesus? How did they know this was the real King of the Jews when they had so easily dismissed Herod? Was there in that Bethlehem encounter a sense of a 'deep underlying silence leading into a sort of helplessness before God'? Did they too find themselves 'being gently eased away from [their] own preoccupation, and so made aware of a twofold otherness – the great swell of worship all around, creation praising God, and ulti-

mately the Son praising the Father; and the mysterious
reality beyond or ahead, drawing that praise out'? In a
tiny house in a small village in an insignificant province
of a mighty empire, did these men feel the whole of
creation crowding in with them to glimpse the God
who made them and who would recreate them and all
things when he worshipped his Father on a wooden
cross, and left a grave empty for good as his life of
praise ended death for ever?

So often we presume these stories work the other
way round: we understand, so we worship. But is
Rowan not right to make us look again, to discover that
when we worship, we understand? The leper worships
Jesus, then sees him as one who can heal; Jairus
worships Jesus, then sees him as one who can raise his
daughter to life; the disciples see Jesus walking on
water, but only as they worship are their eyes of faith
opened to recognise him as God's Son; the Canaanite
woman asks for mercy, but only as she worships does
she realise the depths of her helplessness and her need
for God; the women running away from the empty
tomb are filled with fear – till they see Jesus and worship
him, and suddenly fear leaves and faith comes to stay.

Is this not the story of John in the book of Revelation?
He is on Patmos, imprisoned for his faith, in a world
where although he *knows* Jesus is Lord, most of the
evidence around him seems to point the other way.
Then, as he worships on the Lord's day, heaven opens,
the Lord speaks and the deeper reality is revealed: many
claim power, but they are false; many require worship,

but they are wrong; many think they are in control, but they are wind and smoke. There is a throne in heaven, and someone is seated on it. He has power, he is to be worshipped, he is in control. As John worships, he understands.

Worshipping God makes things clear because it is putting the whole universe back the right way up. We are made to worship him. When we do so, everything else should fall into place. When we fail to understand, perhaps we should pause in our schemes and worries, and worship God for a while.

The Engraver's Story

Phil Lawson Johnston is a well-known songwriter and worship leader. He was part of the early days of renewal at Holy Trinity Brompton, the Alpha church, before moving with his family to Oxford in the late 1980s. Those who know of him primarily for such songs as 'We will magnify' or 'Jesus is the name we honour' may not know that by trade he is actually a glass engraver. Next time you enter HTB, stop to admire the glass doors, which are Phil's handiwork.

One time I was at a conference where we were worshipping and singing the words 'I'm in love with you, for you have called me child'. I had a strong sense that these words were particularly for a woman in the row in front of me – she was trembling, tears were flowing. I had another sense that I should lay my hands on her shoulders and pray for her. I prayed that the Father would hold her in his arms like a baby. I felt she had been deprived of this, and prayed, 'Father, make up the years.'

I spoke to her later and discovered that she had been abused for years by her stepfather and beaten by her mother. She had never allowed a man to pray for her, let alone lay a hand on her in prayer. Actually, those next to her had thought she would freak out when they saw me laying my hands on her shoulders!

She said that at that moment she began to allow her heavenly Father to heal her wounded heart. It was not at all a complete healing, but it was a start.

I'm fascinated by two parts of this story. First, by Phil hearing God speak as he worshipped him, and then by seeing the beginnings of the woman's healing through Phil speaking those words to her as the worship continued around them. Phil always talks of having a 'sense' of God saying something; he does not claim to hear voices as such. But still these senses move him to do something. Now we do have to be careful when we act on these impulses, as we can be wrong, and we must be sure that what we are doing is in line with Scripture – I agree with those who want to remind us of these caveats. Yet I am excited by Phil's story because it seems to me to exactly follow the example Matthew sets us. When we worship, we hear Jesus speak. Sure, the guys in the Gospel stories do have the physical Jesus present with them, but the people Matthew was writing for did not. They had the Holy Spirit, as we do, but not the physical presence of Jesus. Now I have said before that quite clearly Matthew is writing in the way he does, so that his hearers can see what Jesus did with people during his earthly life in order to understand how he relates to them now, and how they should relate to him. This is the reason I am picking up on these worship stories — stories that only Matthew picks out as worship events. Why is worship important in these stories? Because worship is generally important, sure. But also, and maybe primarily, because Matthew knows that his readers and hearers will mainly meet God head-on in worship. As they worship Jesus they will meet him, sense him, learn from him, understand him, hear him speak and grow to be more like him.

When does the Canaanite woman hear Jesus address her? When she worships. When does Jesus speak to James and John's mother? When she worships him. The link is clear. Matthew teaches through his stories that when we worship Jesus, we hear him speak to us. It is as if a key to pastoral care for God's people is unlocked in the act of worship — and why not? Where else should pastoral care begin but in the presence of the Good Shepherd? 'My sheep listen to my voice; I know them, and they follow me,' says Jesus (John 10:27).

So Phil was worshipping, and as he did so he had a sense of the words of the particular song being important for the woman in front of him. Now here is where many of us blow it. We get such a sense and dismiss it. But Phil was obedient to what he perceived to be God's voice, and he acted upon it. He didn't know the dangers; he didn't know that the people with the woman expected a fracas. He only knew it seemed to be the right thing to do. Was this foolhardy? Maybe. But it was also spot on.

In the parable of the unmerciful servant, the title character gets a lot of things right. He worships the king, and through this act of worship, of belittling himself and exalting the king, he receives forgiveness. So far so good. But then he fails to do anything with his newfound state. He carries on as normal. He lives with no sense of the enormity of the change he has benefited from impinging on his life, changing him again. He sees another slave and has no mercy, and that failure to become like the one who forgave him – that failure to act according to the mercy he was shown – condemns him.

We worship God. We receive mercy. We know what the Lord has done for us. Generally, we know of our forgiveness and the way to the Father being opened up through the cross of Christ and, specifically, we know of those many moments in our lives where Jesus has stepped in and made all the difference. But are we truly different as a result? Do these moments of mercy, these breakthroughs in worship, these revelations of the eternal, shape and reshape us, the way we are with others, the way we act when we sense God requiring something of us?

Worshipping God should change us. It should change our understanding of God and our response to him – our willingness to step out in faith and obedience. Phil stepped out. He spoke to the woman, prayed for her and put a hand on her shoulder as he did so, and the Lord used such obedience in the place of worship and began a transformation that may have been incomplete, but that already astounded those who were with the woman and knew how she would usually have reacted to such an action. Phil wasn't making it up. He wasn't imposing his theological worldview on somebody else. He wasn't just using a technique he'd picked up at some conference (though when I said this to him, he replied that he had been very tempted to hold his hand just above the woman's shoulders, as he had seen at a conference, but then he sensed God say quite strongly that he should actually touch her). So he did what he felt was right, what he sensed God would have him do. He was worshipping Jesus, listening to Jesus, being obedient to Jesus, and as a result somebody else was blessed beyond their expectations.

Personally, I find it interesting that the story he tells involves a song I have to confess I don't get on well with. But these songs are used by God whether we like them or not, and just to shame me and make this point particularly well, Paul Thompson also has a story about another song that will never be one of my favourites. He says:

This story is one of forgiveness and reconciliation. I was at a New Wine conference in 1991. During a worship time led by Bryn Haworth one evening we sang some songs that concentrated on the fatherhood of God. I was especially affected by the song 'Father, I can call you Father' by

Danny Daniels. As we sang the song I was more and more troubled by calling God my Father. I began to realise that I was having difficulties because of a long standing problem I had with my own earthly father. Because of something he did just before I went to university, he had caused hurt which affected the whole family, and I had never really forgiven him. As we sang the song I just knew that my unforgiveness was a great weight of sin that I could not carry any longer, and I wept like I have never wept before. I promised there and then that I would write to my dad and tell him I forgave him and I told my wife what I would do, so I would be held accountable. My dad and I have got on really well ever since. The past is forgiven. Hallelujah!

As Paul worshipped, the Lord spoke, and the words he was singing turned themselves around and opened up Paul's heart. The words he sang became God's words to him, and spoke of a different relationship. Just as James and John's mother's request for power and authority in the kingdom of God had turned into a prayer for a quite different power – the spiritual service that is the true mark of spiritual authority – so these words of worship developed a new life, and as Paul sang them, he had to mean them not only to God, but in a way that would demand obedience and a change of heart. When he started that song, and for that matter when he had sung that song previously, his relationship with his human father had been quite far from his thoughts. This time the Lord spoke, and Paul's life was changed again.

J. B. Torrance sees this link as self-evident. If worship draws us into the presence of God, surely it draws us into the character of God? If Jesus relates both to the other members of the Trinity and to us in particular ways, then as we are drawn into him, we too will take on his characteristics, his ways of relating: 'As in worship, so also in our personal relationships with one another, we are given the gift of participating through the Spirit in the incarnate Son's communion with the Father, in the Trinitarian life of God.'[6] Torrance goes on to suggest that this is one of the gifts of holy communion. It draws us into communion with God and each other at the same time, changing all our relationships, making us more fully human than we are at any other time. I would want to agree that this is a part of the richness of communion, but I would also want to add that all worship of God should be doing this. This certainly seems to be part of Matthew's teaching to his early church audience.

The Doctor's Story

Neil Smith is a doctor based in south London. I first knew him as a medical student at Oxford, when he joined a worship band I was leading in our church at that time. Since then he has been involved in worship leading in Anglican and more recently Vineyard congregations. His story comes from the early days of his time with the Sutton Vineyard church.

------

6. J. B. Torrance, *Worship, Community and the Triune God*, p. 28.

In the early days of our church, we would meet together on a Wednesday evening once a month for praise and ministry. Only about 20 or 30 people came to the meetings, but all were hungry for whatever God had for them. Worship was usually led by a single person or by a small unsophisticated band of three or four musicians. On one such evening I was leading. The short practice before the meeting had been unremarkable, there was no sense of great things to come, only the desire among the band to be obedient to God's calling on us to lead worship, and to get on and do it as best we could. It had been a busy day at work, and some of us had got home late and dashed out again quickly to make it to the meeting. There had been no time to grab a bite to eat, never mind to get all worked up and over-excited about the evening ahead. While the pastor was finishing his coffee and calling the meeting to order, we said a quick prayer to ask for anointing in a huddle behind him. I can't remember exactly the words that were said – they were nothing special, I'm certain – but as we took our places ready to start to play I was aware of a tremendous sense of the presence of God in the room. Everyone in the room was aware of the presence of the Holy Spirit, and we stood in silence for several minutes and worshipped God as he touched our hearts and met with us. Nothing about that experience of God could have been 'whipped up' or artificially manipulated by the music because we were completely silent. Eventually when we did begin to sing, the sense of the presence of the Spirit of God became even more tangible, and many people were prophesied over and ministered to.

We probably expect to enjoy awe-inspiring times of worship when we attend conferences led by professional musicians and famous international worship leaders. However, the wonderful thing I have discovered is that God is just as able to meet with us in a profound way through the smaller, less sophisticated gatherings in our churches on a Sunday. It seems to have much less to do with how well we sing or play (i.e. what sound comes out) than with our attitude when we sing or play (i.e. what thought we put in). Whenever I am tempted to congratulate myself on my 'performance' as a worship leader, I do well to remember that God does not need me to play or sing at all to be manifest. The Creator of the universe is not restricted by what we can do for him, or how well we do it. He will do what he will do. More than musicianship, more than anything else, we simply need to try to be obedient to that divine will.

Now Neil is an excellent musician, and his reflections on that Wednesday evening event come from his perspective as a worship leader in his church's tradition. I include them because I'm sure that many people will both agree with his comments and be challenged by them. Obedience to God brings blessing in all areas of our Christian lives, perhaps especially in worship.

But the aspect of this story I would like to focus on for a moment is the surprise of the presence of God in worship. Neil is absolutely right about this. I'm sure most of us have had the same experience of being involved in leading or attending a worship service when our hearts have been far from the throne room of God and closer to the dining room of home or the bedroom of fatigue. And yet, in our weakness, God has been

surprisingly strong. On a day when we expected nothing, we received too much. When I first knew Neil, and
we were in a worship band together, I was constantly
struggling with a fierce depression that seemed to get
the better of me for months on end. And yet week in
week out, as we led worship in our church, God blessed
his people mightily. Just as in Neil's story, people were
spoken to through the worship and through prophetic
words, sick people were prayed for and some got well.
And it had nothing to do with how well I was doing my
job. It was just the grace of God.

We should not be so surprised at this surprise of
worship – this way that God makes himself known to us,
even when we are not looking. Yet we are. I think it is
because we are so aware of our own shortcomings and
the poverty of our own situation that we forget about
how big God is, and how great are the riches of his
grace. We look at ourselves and forget to look up. The
amazing thing is that even when we forget to look up,
God looks down on us and comes to our aid. Was it
when we realised that we needed a Saviour that Jesus
came and died on a cross to restore us to a right life of
worship with God? No. One of my favourite texts in the
New Testament is Romans 5:8: 'God demonstrates his
own love for us in this: While we were still sinners,
Christ died for us.' When we had our backs turned and
were walking off in the wrong direction, God sent his
Son to die for us. Amazing. Does God change? No. So if
we only come to him in the first place because he came
for us, should not this principle continue through all our

Christian lives? Yes. And if that is so, why are we surprised when God shows up in our worship; when we can feel the intangible; when the transcendent becomes immanent? Beats me.

But some argue that this is presuming upon God, and we shouldn't do so. Of course we should be surprised when he rescues us and meets with us and does the stuff in his own power and without our aid. To expect him just to show is to fail to value him. All I can say to that is that knowing and trusting the character of God is not the same as presuming upon him.

I watched an old episode of *ER* this week. There was a drug addict who kept coming back to the ER for treatment, but who refused to go into rehab. She just kept using the doctors and nurses to get her through her latest crisis without ever wanting to address the basic problems in her life. She knew they would help – they had to. But their care of her became more and more superficial. In the end, Carter, not yet a qualified doctor, sat on the steps and poured out his concerns to Lewis: 'These people come in here on drugs and booze and they don't listen to us, and we're supposed to treat them . . . Well, what good is it? Tomorrow they're going to be back on the street doing the same thing. The day after that they're going to be back in here doing the same thing to us.' And Susan Lewis replied, 'It's our job.'[7] Carter felt people were presuming upon his good character; his colleague and friend pointed out

---

7. *ER*, copyright Warner Bros Television, 1996.

that it was their job. These people were not coming to him, but to the doctor, which happened to be him.

Now some people feel that those who keep coming to God to use him for a pick-me-up or a quick fix without taking on the commitments and standards of the Christian life are just like that drug addict, and why should we teach that they can keep coming to God, and he will keep coming to meet them? Because the difference is that God is not like the ER. He is not a hospital casualty department. He is not a tired doctor at the end of his tether. He has no personal problems that keep his mind from listening to us. He is not suffering from lack of sleep and therefore missing obvious things about us or paying us scant attention. And even if we are like that wretched patient, concerned more with the symptoms of our lives and not the root problems, God remains true to his character. He doesn't brush us off. Why not? Because it's not just a job for him; it's a question of who he is – and he is faithful and true, loving and just, compassionate and merciful, all-knowing, all-seeing, all-powerful, always right, always right with us, always right for us. He does not change. God with us. God for us. He may well surprise us and cure us of all sorts of things we thought we had hidden well away as we worship him, because in worship God opens our hearts to him and then has this knack of performing open heart surgery. Knowing this is not presumption; it is faith. It is the faith of those in the boat tossed by the sea and the storm who see Jesus make a difference and worship him, kissing the feet that walk on the water, crying out, 'Who is this that even the wind and the waves obey him?'

Worship opens our eyes to see the truth. We are tired, feel far from God, expect little of him. But he knows this, and still he loves us. So he meets with us, uses us in his service, blesses us, and through us many others. Because it is about him. Worship is about God. We think that because we do it, we are the subject. But this is completely wrong. God is always the subject, always the important thing, always the focus of worship. So he leads us, guides us, blesses us and meets with us. He surprises us, because we would never be so good. God forbid that our worship should be about us. What a travesty that would be, and what a let-down.

Neil is in the room with 20 or 30 others. They say a quick prayer, as if it all depends on them. And before they can play a note or sing a word, the Lord fills the place and they are reminded that it is not about them. It's about Jesus.

My story

I hope that you have seen what these stories have been doing – pulling out issues raised by the Matthew worship stories and showing the truths behind the gospel accounts to apply to our worship today. The follow-on has to be that we must seek when we organise public worship to allow room for these sorts of things to be going on, and we must encourage the kind of private worship that responds to the God who is like this and loves his people so fully. We can't guarantee healing miracles, but we can worship a God who heals and so open up the option in people's hearts of coming to God to ask for his help.

I've filled the pages of this book with little stories of my own, but as we come to the end of this chapter, allow me the indulgence of a longer tale; an account of God changing my life as I worshipped him.

Just before I took my finals at university, I turned over in bed one day and felt my back go 'ping'. Actually, I was praying in bed at the time, so maybe I was being taught a lesson about laziness! I'd had a bad back since my mid-teens – the kind of pain that is a constant discomfort. I couldn't sit or even stand still comfortably; I had to move around to ease the discomfort. But this pain was different. This was severe pain. For the next year I 'suffered a great deal under the care of many doctors' (Mark 5:26), none of whom could trace the problem. I had regular physiotherapy, which alleviated the pain, but did not solve it. Then a very generous lady in my church paid for me to see a chiropractor, and he took X-rays that located the problem at the base of my spine. My GP looked at the X-rays and agreed. The bones at the base of my spine were bent in on each other, not evenly spaced. Moreover they were mis-shaped, and my GP felt that it was possible the whole problem had its roots in a kind of bone disease I might have had in my mid-teens.

Well, people prayed for me and nothing happened. To be honest, I developed an allergy to people praying for my back because there was so much expectation with so little result. I just learned to live with the pain. When I went to theological college, they put me in a room in the attic, 65 steps above street level. Some days each step was agony.

That first Christmas at Wycliffe Hall, the theological college I attended, every time I worshipped God I felt him tell me to have someone pray for my back. I was, as I said, fed up with people praying for me and nothing happening, so I ignored this prompting. Mercifully for me, though I tried not to listen, the Lord continued to speak. Then one evening in January, when I was playing in a worship group for a student service, as we came to the end of one song, a doctor in the congregation came forward to say something he felt the Lord had given him. I remember thinking I should stand aside from my microphone to let him speak. He said, 'Don't stand aside, but receive your healing.'

The words were just what I'd been thinking, and they really struck me. I insisted that some friends pray with me as soon as we got back to Wycliffe. And as they prayed, I experienced the most excruciating pain in my back — it felt as if the bones were moving against each other. My friends asked me as they watched my back, 'Are you doing that?' All I knew was that I was in so much pain I could barely whisper the word 'no'. They carried on praying, one of them putting his hand exactly on the painful spot. Everything got hot. And then the pain stopped.

I could stand still without discomfort. I could sit

evenly without redistributing my weight from one side to the other. Walking felt like walking on air, because there was no pain. I could even sit on one of the pews in the college chapel without pain – now that was remarkable! I climbed those 65 steps to my room pain free. Over a decade on, there is still no pain.

Sometimes I shudder to think that I nearly didn't have anyone pray for me, but that night as we worshipped, the Lord spoke to someone else and they spoke to me, and in that place of worship I knew it was the Lord. And he healed me.

I'm reminded of a song we used to sing in my junior school assemblies. I can still remember the words:

> Tell me the stories of Jesus I long to hear;
> Things I would ask him to tell me, if he were here.
> Scenes by the wayside, tales by the sea,
> Stories of Jesus – tell them to me.
>
> *William H. Parker, 1885*

If he were here. But this is the great thing about worship: when we worship Jesus, he *is* here. He's always here, sure, but when we worship him, we see it's true. As true as it was for the wise men, for the leper, for Jairus, for the disciples in the boat, for the Canaanite woman, for Zebedee's wife, for the women at the tomb, for the apostles receiving the Great Commission. Matthew teaches us that what was true for these people is true for us. What they experienced in worship, we can experience in worship. The God they met as they worshipped is the God we meet as we worship. Same God, same worship, new lives changed and transformed. Our lives.

And then Matthew reaches his climax – his telling of the story of the crucifixion – and all the theory and all the stories come together.

8

The Big Picture

Little child, for you Jesus Christ has come, he has fought, he has suffered. For you he entered into the shadow of Gethsemane and the horror of Calvary. For you he uttered the cry, 'It is finished!' For you he rose from the dead and ascended into heaven and there he intercedes – for you, little child, even though you do not know it. But in this way the word of the gospel becomes true. 'We love him, because he first loved us.'[1]

Take heart, my friends, the end is in sight! This book has been concerned with seeing worship as the big picture in life. In order for that to hold true, we have had to do some serious theological work, enabling us to

---

1. From the baptism liturgy of the French Reformed Church, quoted in J. B. Torrance, *Worship, Community and the Triune God of Grace*, p. 65.

see where the big ideas of our faith connect with
worshipping God. In Chapter 1 we looked at the question of sin, and saw that biblically speaking the main
issue is all about getting worship right or wrong –
worshipping God our Creator or worshipping some
other created thing. We know the cross is the answer to
sin, but in Chapter 2 we had to see how the cross was
about worship; how the words used in the New
Testament to describe what Jesus did there come from
Jewish temple worship services and festivals. Chapter 3
took us through the nature of the word 'Lord', to help
us understand some of the content of our own worship
of God and to deepen our appreciation of what we do.
In Chapter 4 we looked at how worship shapes and
defines our whole Christian experience. Then we set our
attention on Matthew's Gospel, exploring the worship
stories scattered throughout the Gospel, and we spent a
further three chapters looking at some of my earlier
ideas in the context of Jesus' life and ministry, and in the
experience of people today.

But now as we approach the end of this book, I want
us to step back; to move our focus away from the detail
and back to the big picture; to see the Perfect
Worshipper expressing perfect worship at the cross. The
Bible puts the worship of God firmly at the centre of the
Christian life and Christian doctrine, and in my opinion
the clearest place to find this comes in the way Matthew
closes his account of Jesus' life, death and resurrection.
The last three chapters of Matthew's Gospel take us
through all these ideas, wrapping them around the

concept of worship, as he has done with so much of his teaching throughout his book. This chapter of my book is simply going to follow his lead. What we are about to see together is simply a clear run-through of the worship question as Matthew presents it at the end of his Gospel; the conclusion and summation of everything that has gone before.

Some ointment, some bread, empty words and a cup of suffering (Matthew 26:1–46)

Matthew begins his account of the death of Jesus with a series of sharply observed vignettes – little stories with great meaning, filled with contrasts, comparisons and contradictions.

The first is the tale of a woman who comes to the home of Simon the Leper, where Jesus is eating with his disciples. Sorry – Simon the ex-Leper. They wouldn't be in the house otherwise. So the very setting of the story tells us of Jesus' power, and his compassion for people ruled by sickness and sin. He's here to make a difference.

Anyway, the woman comes in, ignores all the disciples, goes straight to Jesus and pours this expensive ointment (or perfume in some translations) all over his head as he is there eating the meal. And I do mean expensive. This isn't just your average Superdrug aftershave. Mark gives the price at 300 denarii, about a year's wages for your average unskilled Jewish labourer. Thousands of pounds' worth. Some ointment.

The disciples can't get over it. Indignantly they ask, 'Why this waste? This perfume could have been sold at a high price and the money given to the poor.' But Jesus disagrees: 'She has done a beautiful thing to me. The poor you will always have with you, but you will not always have me . . . she did it to prepare me for burial . . . wherever this gospel is preached . . . what she has done will also be told, in memory of her.'

Why? Why is this story so special? Because this gospel is about worshipping Jesus. This is the good news. Once we were trapped in a world of sin, far from God, wanting to worship because it's the way we are made, but ending up worshipping all the wrong things, getting further and further from God. But now, thanks to what Jesus has done for us, we can worship in spirit and in truth. We can be forgiven the stain of idolatry and can enter into a right relationship where we, the created, worship God the Creator. And everything we have is poured out for him in gratitude and worship. We hold nothing back, because everything is his. What a joy worshipping Jesus is. Our eyes don't focus on the things of this world any more, because Jesus fills our vision. Pounds and pence fade and rust and are forgotten, for now we have discovered real value, real treasure. This woman got it right before the event, before the cross. She looked forward with the eyes of faith. Now that's a story to be told, says Jesus.

But straight away, Matthew takes us elsewhere. Real value and real worship are forgotten. Is the attitude of the disciples and this woman the first real contrast

Matthew draws here? Maybe. But it isn't half as sharp as the comparison he draws with Judas, who instead of pouring out his life's savings on the head of his life's Saviour, sells that head for 30 pieces of silver (the value of a slave in Exodus 21 and the pay of a shepherd in Zechariah 11). Some worship books will tell you that our word 'worship' comes from an Anglo-Saxon word that meant literally 'worth-ship'; giving or ascribing worth to something. Well, on that count the woman with the ointment wins the prize. And Judas gets worship all wrong.

George Herbert, the seventeenth-century clergyman and poet, put it this way:

> Mine own apostle, who the bag did bear,
> Though he had all I had, did not forbear
> To sell me also and to put me there:
> Was ever grief like mine?
>
> For thirty pence he did my death devise,
> Who at three hundred did the ointment prize,
> Not half so sweet as my sacrifice:
> Was ever grief like mine?[2]

It starts here. We are going to see that just as wrong worship, the root of all sin, was the theological reason for the death of Jesus, so wrong worship was the actual cause of his death. This is not just the theory, says

---

2. George Herbert, 'The Sacrifice' in *The Temple*, section two, 'The Church', stanzas 4 and 5.

Matthew; it's the practice. It's not just a neat idea; it is what actually happened. Wrong worship took Jesus to the cross. And it starts here, with one of the twelve – the man who carried the common purse, Judas. A man who knew his own price but not his master's worth.

They sit at table in the city, that last evening they all spent together. Jesus says that one of them will betray him. 'Surely not I, Lord?' they reply one by one around the room. Matthew holds no suspense for us. He has already told us the guilty party. Twenty-two innocent eyes open wide as they speak to their Lord. How can they betray their Lord, when so much is invested in that very title? The character of the man, the very character of God; the power of the man, bringing healing and life to the sick and the dead; the way he always intervenes for them – when they couldn't feed a crowd, when the sea turned stormy, when things got out of control and they were attacked by demoniacs.

Two eyes are not so wide. The mouth below them asks a different question: 'Surely not I, Rabbi?' Eleven disciples name Jesus as Lord; one calls him 'Rabbi'. True, they will all forget soon enough that he is Lord, but one disciple has already forgotten. Forgotten his character. Forgotten his power. Forgotten his promise to intervene. Forgotten to name him as Lord. Rabbi – teacher – will do. Eleven will fall, but their hearts belong to God. They have chosen their Lord, and they have chosen well. They will also rise again, shortly, after Jesus' resurrection, and they will again follow their Lord. But one has made a different decision. His worship is elsewhere.

His life will bear the results of his choice.

Then Jesus takes some bread and some wine and gives it to his disciples. In the midst of the unfolding story he creates another story; a story that will be the way the church remembers and retells the great story. He defines the church's corporate worship: it's about a body, it's about giving thanks, it's about being broken, it's about Jesus. And it's about blood – the stuff of life; about a promise and a calling; about forgiveness; about his Father's kingdom.

Of course worship is about these things. All our worship, whether we meet around the Lord's table, the pastor's Bible, Mrs Jones's kitchen sink or the youth leader's guitar. But here's a thing: in the account of the Last Supper, only Matthew has the line about forgiveness. It's not there in Mark. Luke doesn't have it. John doesn't tell the story this way. Paul's account in 1 Corinthians omits it. So why does Matthew include the line 'for the forgiveness of sins'?

Let's go back. What is sin? Well, back in Chapter 1 we asked the same question a different way round. What is the first commandment? To love God; to put him first; to worship him and him alone. So what is sin? Sin is breaking the command. And the command is? To love God; to worship him. So sin is? Not loving and worshipping God. So what needs to be forgiven? Not loving and worshipping God. Jesus says, in the course of the meal that establishes the pattern for 2,000 years of Christian worship services, that he will pour out his blood for us as a promise that we will be forgiven our sins, our wrong worship that ruins our lives. It's not just a promise, a covenant. It's a New Covenant, as Jeremiah foretold (Jeremiah 31:31–34):

> 'The time is coming,' declares the Lord, 'when I will make a new covenant with the house of Israel and with the house of Judah . . . This is the covenant that I will make with the house of Israel after that time,' declares the Lord. 'I will put my law in their minds and write it on their hearts. I will be their God, and they will be my people. No longer will a man teach his neighbour, or a man his brother, saying, "Know the Lord," because they will all know me, from the least of them to the greatest,' declares the Lord. 'For I will forgive their wickedness and will remember their sins no more.'

The New Covenant is about worship. It is about past wickedness and sin being forgiven (the way we used to worship anything and everything but God that lies at the heart of all other sin and wickedness). And instead, in our minds and hearts will live the law of God. And where does the law of God start? With the command to love and worship God. That love and worship of God will come from within under the New Covenant. It will not be a matter of external rules and regulations that have to be taught and enforced. 'They will all know me,' says the Lord. And Jesus adds, '. . . through my blood, poured out for you.' The New Covenant command is not 'Worship!' or 'Love!' but 'Worship God! Love God!'

A friend of mine, Clare, asked me how God could

command us to worship him. Surely we have to choose to do that or it is invalid? But this is the whole point. We have no choice because it is the way we are made: we will worship, we will love. It's just that under the old system, the way things work outside of the forgiveness Christ wins for us by getting worship ultimately and conclusively right on the cross, we worship and love the wrong things. The excitement of the New Covenant, the news that is good, is that now we can get worship right by worshipping the right person: all the sin of the past is blown away for those who trust in Jesus. The commands of God to love him and worship him alone are suddenly in our hearts and minds, as natural as can be. It's a remarkable change. An amazing gift.

Let's not settle for a superficial reading of our Bibles, where the only worship reference in the events around the crucifixion comes in Matthew 28:30: 'When they had sung a hymn'. All of these things take place during the Passover; the whole setting is a week-long worship festival. As I said way back in Chapter 1, Passover is Spring Harvest, New Wine, Soul Survivor and any other worship festival you care to mention rolled into one and celebrated slap bang in the middle of the nation's capital city. The contrast of the use of the word 'Lord' by the eleven and 'Rabbi' by Judas sets up the worshippers against the betrayer. The establishing of the Last Supper puts the story into the regular life of Christian worship, and the forgiveness of sins is fundamentally about addressing the heart of wrong worship that must be changed before God's wayward people can be changed into worthy members of the body of Christ.

And how that forgiveness is needed. Jesus says that the eleven will all fall away, and Peter protests that he never will. But his words are empty. Say what you mean, Peter, and mean what you say. When Jesus goes to pray in Gethsemane, he takes Peter and James and John to pray with him. Jesus faces up to the cost of obedience. True worship. Perfect worship. Giving God everything, no matter what the cost. He asks for an easier way, but accepts the path God shows him. Then he turns and sees his closest friends asleep, unaware of his agony. Peter's proud promises never to let his master down are already just so many empty words; Jesus' cup of suffering is filling to the brim, ready for the drinking.

The kiss of death (Matthew 26:47–56)

Remember our worship word? *Proskuneo* – literally, 'I come towards to kiss'; figuratively, 'to bow before or to pay obeisance; to acknowledge one greater than you'. From there it comes to mean 'to worship'. It is the word Matthew has used all along for worship. Just keep it in mind.

For now the betrayer comes, with a crowd of others carrying swords and clubs and torches and lanterns through the night. And he has arranged a signal with the crowd, so that in the press of the throng and the dark of the hour they should not take the wrong man. His signal? He will come towards and kiss Jesus. The act of worship. The description of the worship word. But this will not be worship. This will be the very definition of sin. Listen to the words of George Herbert again:

> Arise, arise, they come. Look how they run.
> Alas what haste they make to be undone!
> How with their lanterns do they seek the sun!
> Was ever grief like mine?

> Judas, dost thou betray me with a kiss?
> Canst thou find hell about my lips? And miss
> Of life, just at the gates of life and bliss?
> Was ever grief like mine?[3]

Worship brings life, but what Judas does is death. It is a mockery, a fraud, a betrayal of everything Jesus was preparing to give. Herbert puts it brilliantly: Judas finds 'hell about my lips' in an act that should be 'the gates of life and bliss'.

Matthew emphasises the point by the word he uses for 'kiss'. He avoids the *kuneo* word and chooses instead *phileo*. What is the difference? *Kuneo* is the kiss of a lesser to a greater. *Phileo* is the kiss of equals. It comes from the word meaning 'brotherly love; the love of friends'. Indeed, the word *phileo* is only translated as 'kiss' in this story; otherwise it is used for 'I love'.

Matthew is describing the act of the worship word, but making it as clear as he can that this is not worship. It is anything but. Yes, Judas comes towards Jesus to kiss

---

3. George Herbert, stanzas 9 and 11.

him, but this is no reverential kiss of worship. This is rather a kiss of presumption; of failing to see who Jesus is; of refusing to grant him his proper place. Or perhaps there is an even darker interpretation. Perhaps he does see who Jesus is; he does see the Father in the face of the Son. And this refusal to bow, to be less, is in fact a claiming to be equal to God ('I know who you are, and I am every bit as good as you, matey'). Judas falls for the same temptation that the serpent offered Adam and Eve in the garden: 'You can be like God!' The way Judas speaks to Jesus pushes the point home. He still calls him 'Rabbi', not 'Lord'; he either does not or will not see, or simply refuses to acknowledge what the other eleven gladly affirm – the lordship of this Jesus. His 'worship' is so wrong, so black, that one almost feels polluted by it just on reading the words that describe it.

Except, haven't we all been there? Doesn't it make you stop in your tracks to realise that when we slip into being too matey with Jesus, we are emulating Judas? Jesus is very near – this is the promise of God, the gift of God – but God's gifts are to be received with awe and thanksgiving, not taken for granted. There is a fine line between resting in the promises and rotting in the presumption.

And you know when I said that in the stories that involve worship, Matthew introduces the word *proskuneo* when Mark does not have that word, to make the point that these people really are worshipping Jesus? It works the other way too. Matthew will only use this word for true worship, so when the guards mock Jesus after the trial, Mark says they 'worshipped Jesus', but Matthew says only that they 'knelt before' him (Mark 15:19; cf. Matthew 27:29). It wasn't worship. So it doesn't get the word. But do not think that because Matthew avoids the *proskuneo* word here the concept is absent. Anything but.

This is what takes Jesus to the cross, and this is why this act is known as the betrayal. After all, Peter will deny Jesus and the other ten will run away. Is that not betrayal too? No, not in the same league. Here is the God who comes to be a man to help people worship in spirit and in truth, and here is the man who worships in falsity and betrayal and who sends him to the cross. The reason Jesus came to die is the reason he is sent to his death. Wrong worship betrays the one who comes to get worship right and to open up a new world of right relationship to God for all through his perfect worship. It was wrong worship in Eden, wrong worship in Israel, wrong worship in all the earth and wrong worship in Gethsemane that took Jesus to the cross.

The sickness spreads (Matthew 26:57 – 27:44)

Long ago, one man and one woman were responsible for one act of wrong worship that turned the world upside down. Now, although Judas is a focus for similar sin, the sickness spreads, and Matthew takes us through all the players in the story in order to show us that wrong worship is now the common sin. Everybody is guilty here.

The first group to be put under the spotlight are the chief priests and the whole Sanhedrin, the Jewish council in Jerusalem, and their highest court of justice. Not that there was much justice on show that night. We spent some time a couple of chapters ago working through the idea that worship is not just a matter of words, but of meaning what we say, of living a life that lives up to the words we sing, of walking the walk as we talk the talk. So we worship a God of justice – then let us be just. We worship a God of truthfulness – then let us be true. We worship a God of mercy – then let us be merciful. We worship a God of love – then let us be loving, loving our neighbour as ourselves. Worship is the entire Godward response of our lives, focused in the corporate expression. The corporate expression without the whole life is a sham and a charade.

The night before Jesus died, the men responsible for the worship of Israel and charged with executing God's justice, including the high priest (the man who alone could enter the Holy of Holies once a year), taught the whole world that the best forms of worship in the world count for nothing unless they change the heart. Worse, they showed that when we feel our patterns of worship to be threatened we can be so blinded by how we worship that we completely fail to see who we worship. Being responsible for the worship of Israel, these men thought only of themselves. Being charged with executing God's justice, they decided to execute God's Son. Being honoured to enter into the presence of God, they charged the Word of God with words of blasphemy. All they had was false witnesses, meaningless charges and enough prejudice to blind more eyes than Jesus had opened to date. Forgive me for quoting so much of Herbert's poem, but he does put it well:

> Then from one ruler to another bound
> They lead me; urging, that it was not sound
> What I taught: comments would the text confound.
> Was ever grief like mine?
>
> Then they accuse me of great blasphemy,
> That I did thrust into the Deity,
> Who never thought that any robbery.
> Was ever grief like mine?
>
> Some said, that I the temple to the floor
> In three days razed, and raised as before.
> Why, he that built the world can do much more:
> Was ever grief like mine?[4]

From the beginning of his Gospel, Matthew has kept no secrets from us. This is not a murder mystery, where one only discovers on the last page who did it and why. Matthew spills the beans at the very start. This Jesus is the one we should worship. He is God's Son, sent to redeem us, to atone for our sins, to win forgiveness and to worship the Father so that we may worship him. And that worship will transform the world, bringing in the kingdom of God. Jesus alone is worthy of our worship.

---

4. George Herbert, stanzas 14, 16 and 17.

So what is the Sanhedrin's verdict? 'He is worthy of death.' These men would make Jesus guilty of sin, but Matthew makes the guilt stick on them.

Then he moves on. Peter and Judas come back into the frame. Both are shown to be as guilty as the Sanhedrin of wrong worship, though Matthew makes a point of allowing Peter a ray of hope that Judas never sees.

Peter has the chance to prove true the profession of faith he made earlier in the night. He said he would always stick by Jesus, never disown him, even die with him. So he is given three opportunities to make the good confession, to declare his faith in Jesus, to speak up for his Lord. Bit-part players in the story approach him – a couple of slave girls and the high priest's servant – and ask him if he's with Jesus. He denies it. These people have no power, they pose no real threat to Peter, yet he cannot stand up to them. He cannot stand up for what he believes and whom he believes in.

Compare this with Judas. When he sees that they have condemned Jesus, he is filled with remorse. He does not stand at a distance. He goes straight to the chief priests and the elders. He wastes no time talking to the extras on the set; he goes straight to the main actors in the drama that is unfolding. He doesn't wait for them to speak to him; he speaks to them. And he does not avoid the issue, claim innocence, pretend to be uninvolved. He says quite clearly, 'I have sinned, for I have betrayed innocent blood.' These people Judas speaks to do have power. They could charge Judas alongside Jesus and as easily kill two men as one. But

Judas shows no fear. He makes his confession. He stands up for Jesus. And the men with the power look at him with great disdain and simply reply, 'So what?'

Actually, there is a further level to Peter's denial of Jesus. Not only does he fail to own his Lord, to name him as Lord before others, but in fact it can be argued that he goes as far as to curse Jesus. The closest friend curses his master. Matthew keeps this idea of wrong worship running through this story. In verse 74, where Peter curses himself, the word all modern Bibles translate as 'to call down curses on himself' in fact may mean something altogether darker. The word Matthew uses normally means 'to curse *someone else*'. In context, where the questioners are always referring to Jesus, and Peter replies to them using the words 'the man' to mean Jesus, the most obvious meaning is that Peter calls down curses on Jesus (in the same way that Christians were called to curse Jesus when on trial for their lives under various later pagan regimes). 'If Matthew and Mark have understandably refrained from stating this explicitly, it is the probable implication of the words they have used.'[5] Peter's denial of Jesus is not simply on the level of pretending not to know him. He curses the one he should worship.

And yet Peter and Judas end these little episodes very differently. Peter denies his Lord, curses him even, in front of unimportant people; Judas confesses Jesus' innocence before powerful men. But Judas hangs

5. R. T. France, *Matthew* (IVP, 1985).

himself and Peter merely weeps. Possibly Judas is react-
ing to his greater part in the events that are unfolding –
he handed Jesus over, and finds he cannot undo his evil.
Peter has only uttered evil words. But Matthew has
reminded us so many times of the importance of words
and deeds belonging together that this seems an
unlikely answer. In the Sermon on the Mount Jesus told
his disciples, Judas and Matthew included, that anger is
the same as murder; that calling someone a fool puts
the speaker in danger of hell. Peter's words are a serious
matter. He has cursed God and broken the first
command. He too is guilty of the most grievous sin.

The difference was partly seen back when Peter said,
'Surely not I, Lord?' and Judas said 'Rabbi' instead, but it
also comes in verse 75: 'Then Peter remembered the
word Jesus had spoken.' Matthew is making a case for
the guilt of all humanity as we approach the cross: the
Jews, the Gentiles, the common crowd, the soldiers
under orders and the disciples themselves. Everyone is
guilty. We are guilty. Jesus is on the cross because we
get worship wrong; we put first in our lives anything
and everything except the Lord God who should be
there. Yet Peter stands for all of us who know Jesus and
get this wrong, and Matthew wants us to see that
although what we do is wrong, yet there is hope. Judas
has no hope. The Sanhedrin have no hope. Pilate will
have no hope. But Peter has hope. Because even in his
denial, his betrayal, his cursing of God, he remembers
Jesus' words, and tears of sorrow fill his eyes, grief fills
his heart and already the seeds of repentance are begin-

ning to take root. This is, as I said, no suspense novel. We know the outcome. And even as Matthew builds his climax he gives away the end of all things: when you worship the wrong things and fail to worship God, remember Jesus, remember his words, and know that this is not the end. He forgave Peter and he will forgive you.

From two men who understand that they are responsible for their deeds, we move to another who tries to avoid such responsibility. Pilate meets Jesus. They talk, briefly. Pilate sees that Jesus is innocent and his wife confirms his feeling, but the crowd are baying for blood and Pilate gives in. His actions take us back to the Garden of Eden again. Adam says, 'It wasn't me; it was the woman.' Eve says, 'It wasn't me; it was the serpent.' Pilate says, 'It's not me; it's your decision.' The crowd are eager to take responsibility, but Pilate isn't to be let off so easily. Bishop Graham Cray is very fond of saying that worship is essentially corporate, but always personal. It is not simply about me, but my response matters. Avoiding the issue does not work. Pilate says that it is nothing to do with him, but what does he then do with Jesus? Matthew puts it very clearly: 'He had Jesus flogged, and handed him over to be crucified.' Does Pilate worship Jesus? No. Does he side-step the question? No. He makes his decision: he will go with the crowd. But the responsibility for his actions remains with him alone. *He* has Jesus flogged. *He* hands him over for crucifixion. We cannot avoid the issue of whom we worship, whom we put first, whom we choose to follow and love with all our hearts. We all make the choice, says Matthew.

The picture is building. Matthew places cameo upon cameo, little scenes of great meaning rising one upon the next in order to make us see what took Christ to the cross. And as we draw closer, everything becomes clearer.

For now everyone speaks, everyone has their turn to express themselves. And all of them – soldiers, thieves, passers-by, priests – choose to use the words of worship but not the heart. 'Hail, King of the Jews', 'This is Jesus, King of the Jews', 'The Son of God', 'He saved others', 'the King of Israel', 'He trusts in God – let God rescue him', 'He said, "I am the Son of God"' (Matthew 27:29,37,40,42,43). This is mockery. This is worship gone sour. This is wrong worship at its height and at its depth. Right words, wrong hearts. Time for some more George Herbert:

> See how spite cankers things. These words aright
> Used and wished are the whole world's light:
> But honey is their gall, brightness their night:
> Was ever grief like mine?
>
> Now heal thyself, Physician, now come down.
> Alas! I did so when I left my crown
> And Father's smile for you, to feel his frown:
> Was ever grief like mine?[6]

---

6. George Herbert, stanzas 28 and 56.

Take a look at this, says Matthew. Do you see what took Jesus to the cross? Do you for a moment think it was murder or adultery or gossip or theft or sex before marriage or fraud or tax evasion or selfishness or greed?[7] Look at the scene before you. There is one sin, and the whole world is guilty. And you who organise the people's worship, take care, for good words and bad hearts stand around Calvary like howling dogs.

> What do you think? There was a man who had two sons. He went to the first and said, 'Son, go and work today in the vineyard.'
> 'I will not,' he answered, but later he changed his mind and went.
> Then the father went to the other son and said the same thing. He answered, 'I will, sir,' but he did not go.
> Which of the two did what his father wanted? (Matthew 21:28–31)

Worship is a question of hearts and mouths, words and deeds, working together, being consistent, being true, living out our songs of praise, hearing the words of Jesus and putting them into practice, believing and trusting, loving God and loving our neighbour. And in our own strength it is impossible. We cannot do it. We end up with the mob at Golgotha, condemned by our own lips

---

7. My hyperbole is in danger of carrying me away. Obviously these are sinful things and obviously they matter, but equally obviously they are secondary issues in that the great sin, the root sin, the causal sin, remains the breaking of the first command.

and lives. We say one thing and do another. We get the
words right and the living wrong. We get the living
right but the words wrong. We get the words right but
we don't mean them. We get the lives right – by accident. Remember that Matthew is writing to a worshipping community, not a theological symposium. They
hear these words and hear their own songs too.
They hear what he is saying. They hear their own
poverty and know that their own worship is found
wanting, just as ours is, and they too want a way out, a
way forward, a way beyond the barriers that trip them
up as easily as they trip us. And Matthew has a word for
them and for us. As Neil Smith discovered in that story
of his, and Rowan Williams discovered in that story of
his, it is really so simple. Friends, it's not about us. It's
about Jesus.

Salvation's song (Matthew 27:45–55)

> In healing not myself, there doth consist
> All that salvation which ye now resist;
> Your safety in my sickness doth subsist:
> Was ever grief like mine?[8]

When I was at Wycliffe Hall, training for ordained
ministry, we all had to go on at least one college
mission. I went on one in my first year, to Paddock
Wood in Kent. It was a very exciting week, with a lot

---

8. George Herbert, stanza 57.

happening – especially in the schools. Many people heard about Jesus and several made decisions to become followers of him. I did mostly music and drama during the week, but I had to preach one sermon while there. The mission was in Holy Week 1991, and I was given the sermon on Good Friday. I had not done much preaching at that stage of my life, and I was particularly daunted by the prospect of preaching about the cross to a congregation that included several theological college students. What if I got it wrong? What if they didn't like what I said? What if I preached heresy by mistake? I could only think of a comment made by one of my college tutors, the Orthodox bishop Kallistos Ware, who had told us a story about visiting abroad and reading a newspaper headline that said, 'Bishop preaches heresy.' 'Imagine my horror,' he had said, 'to discover that bishop was me!'

So I made a decision. In all honesty I could not see how the cross worked. I simply did not understand the logic of it – how Jesus dying on a couple of planks of wood should make any difference to my telling lies to a friend to get out of a sticky situation, or any other of my many sins. To me there was a logical gap here. My sin and his solution did not seem to meet. They did not seem to be of the same order – they had no logical connection. Now don't get me wrong. I had no doubt at all that it did work. I just didn't see how it worked. In the end I chose to be honest. I preached that I did not understand how the cross worked, but that I knew it did work, and then I talked about that.

But now I see.

In the midst of a world where worship has gone sour, where people choose to worship that which is not God and to not worship God himself, a world where the first command is forgotten and the rest of the law built upon that command fails because its foundation is corroded and taken away; in the midst of taunts and temptations and mocking and madness, Jesus worships his Father perfectly.

The four Gospels in the New Testament between them record seven things that Jesus said from the cross, often referred to as the seven last words. Matthew has room for only one, perhaps the most misunderstood thing Jesus ever said: 'My God, my God, why have you forsaken me?' This is not just a cry of desperation; of the Son being torn from the Father's bosom by the weight of this world's sin. This is a cry of praise: the perfect Son perfectly worshipping the Father of perfection. Jesus, in the agony of crucifixion, begins to recite Psalm 22. In the final ultimate act of a worshipping life, where all his deeds glorified his Father, he adds the words to go with it. Nailed to the cross, he sings from the songbook of Israel. Indeed, I would argue that all of the seven last words have their origins in this psalm of praise, and just as the crowd failed to get the reference that dark Friday, we still miss it today. Perhaps you would take just a few moments now to read this psalm in full in your Bible.

Jesus begins with the first verse, which does seem to be a desperate cry. But Matthew has not brought us to a place of desperation. He has brought us to see the worship that makes our mouths open wide in awe. He has brought us to see the answer to the mess of sin all around. In creating the atmosphere of false and wrong worship, he provides God's perfect answer by showing us that Jesus remains true even here. All he writes for us is the psalm's opening verse, but as he has referred to many passages of the Old Testament throughout his Gospel, now this too is a reference, incomplete but sending us back to see his point.

You can see why this psalm might be on Jesus' mind as he is crucified. The physical description of crucifixion (written, mind you, some 500 years before crucifixion became a common form of torture) is very precise. But more than that, it speaks of praising God from first to last, and Jesus on the cross is bringing together his final act and its meaning. How many times have we noted that the Bible makes us see that what we do and what we say must go together? The life and the liturgy. The words and the deeds. Jesus does both at Calvary: perfect worship, perfect action, perfect words. His living and his dying sing out salvation's song. The writer to the Hebrews is particularly keen that we get this point because almost his first reference to the cross of Christ (2:9–12) is explained by a quotation from Psalm 22, where the words of the psalm are presented to us as Jesus' own words, despite the fact that none of the Gospel writers actually record Jesus saying them: 'I will declare your name to my brothers; in the presence of the congregation I will sing your praises.' This is his first

image of the cross – Jesus worshipping God in the midst
of his people. And if Psalm 22 is his automatic reference
to that scene, perhaps there is a reason. Let's look at the
seven last words, and see that reason more clearly.

The first word is, as we have already noted, obvious.
It is the first line of the psalm: 'My God, my God, why
have you forsaken me?' (Matthew 27:46; Mark 15:34).
The second, 'Father, forgive them, for they do not know
what they are doing' (Luke 23:34), takes us to verses 6
to 8 of the psalm: the crowd despise him, they reject
him, they hurl insults and say things that they do not
understand about his relationship to God. Jesus hears
the taunts, hears the mocking use of words of worship,
and as he recites them in the psalm, he begs forgiveness
for these people. After all, that is why he is where he is.
These words of forgiveness are not in the psalm, but the
taunting that provokes them is. Indeed, Matthew
quotes the taunting words of the psalm verbatim in
verse 43 of this chapter, though we hear them in the
mouths of the chief priests, teachers of the law and
elders. John does the same with verse 18 of the psalm in
his own Gospel (John 19:24), only this time it is the
soldiers who act out the words. Jesus knows; he understands that this shouting, spitting mess of humanity
does not understand what is going on. But they will.
Father, forgive them!

The third word follows straight away. Verses 9 to 11
of the psalm talk of his mother, and of no one being
there to help. So Jesus looks down from the cross, sees
Mary, and close by her John, and says, 'Dear woman,

here is your son,' and to the beloved disciple he says, 'Here is your mother' (John 19:26). The words he recites remind him of Mary, and he makes certain even at this time that she should not be left with no one to help her in her time of trouble. The psalm in verses 14 to 18 then speaks of the agony of crucifixion – the detail of the physical agony. Jesus sees his bones out of joint, so clear he can count them. He feels the strain on his heart, the intense pain of hands and feet pierced, and in the heat of the day the way his tongue sticks to the roof of his mouth as slowly he dehydrates. 'I am thirsty,' says Jesus (John 19:28).

One of the thieves stops his cursing as he sees the way Jesus dies with such power and purity. He rebukes his fellow criminal who curses still, saying (in Luke's account), 'Don't you fear God?' Then he turns to Jesus and asks that he should not forget him when he goes to this kingdom of his. In verse 25 of the psalm, Jesus promises to fulfil his vows before those who fear God; and this thief, albeit late in his life, has decided to fear God. So here is the vow fulfilled as Jesus recites verse 26: the poor man will eat and be satisfied, the man who seeks the Lord will praise him, his heart will live for ever: 'Today you will be with me in paradise' (Luke 23:43).

Jesus is near the end. Hope is very close now. Verse 24 has reminded him that God has not hidden his face. He is right here, his strong hand ready to help – verse 29 promises feasting and worshipping for all who kneel before God; all who cannot keep themselves alive. Knowing his end to be near, knowing he will not live much longer, Jesus says that this is where he is going; this is the one to whom he is going: 'Father, into your hands I commit my spirit' (Luke 23:46).

And then it ends. This act of perfect worship, done in a world of total sin, comes to an end, and in triumph on that bleak hillside at Golgotha, Jesus utters the final words of the psalm: God has done it; 'It is finished' (John 19:30).

There was another hill, another occasion, crowds milling around as Jesus taught his followers the blessings and commands of Christian living. He taught with authority and power, and some wondered if he was establishing a new law for God's people, or abolishing the old. Jesus answered them:

Do not think that I have come to abolish the Law or the Prophets; I have not come to abolish them but to fulfil them. I tell you the truth, until heaven and earth disappear, not the smallest letter, not the least stroke of a pen, will by any means disappear from the Law until everything is accomplished. (Matthew 5:17–18)

It *is* accomplished. He has done it. The Law starts with the command to worship God, and everything else follows on from that point. This is what we all break. This is what Jesus has fulfilled. He has kept his promise.

Just as the leper caught good health from Jesus' hands, and Jairus' daughter though dead caught life from the Lord of life, now a sinful world catches forgiveness, and Jesus' perfect worship infects the world with worship that is true and holy and right. Wrong worship begins to die. Sin begins to shrivel. The temple curtain is torn in two as the power of what Jesus has done breaks down the barrier between God and his people – the barrier that came from the rule of sin. Jesus' perfect worship is stronger than a whole world of wrong worship, and it begins to assert itself. This is the victory of the cross. The earth shakes and rocks split as the old created order hears its death knell and the new creation begins to rise. Dead people catch life in the wake of the triumph of the Son of God. And though the priests are never recorded as taking back a single word of their blasphemy, the soldiers who had mocked the Messiah turn from their scorn and with almost the same words they had used not hours before now catch this spirit of worship: 'Surely he was the Son of God!'

The gift of worship (Matthew 27:57 – 28:20)

When my grandmother died, I remember one of my uncles phoning my dad. It was a short call, and afterwards Dad came into the front room and said, 'That was Tom, ringing to say he didn't know what to say.' When faced with the great events of life, all too often we have no words. We resort to simple, almost knee-jerk reactions, because they are all we can manage. We don't know what to say. We put the kettle on. We drink strong tea, even if we hate the stuff, because what else is there to do? We walk around like people in a dream, in a daze, not knowing what we are doing.

So Joseph of Arimathea finds Pilate and gets permission to bury the body. He rolls a stone over the entrance to the grave. It's an automatic action – there's a body in there, even if it hasn't been properly prepared for burial. The two Marys sit and watch, numb with grief. The chief priests and Pharisees send a delegation to Pilate on the Sabbath to set up a guard on the tomb – just to make sure. Where everyone else is we don't know. Some are probably at home, staring at nothing. Some are probably in the temple for the end of the Passover week. It's the automatic thing to do: some seeking silent company; others craving solitude; the women waiting for Sabbath to end so they can tend to the body, dress it properly for burial, do their job.

And Matthew reveals how Jesus blows away all these plans, activities, fears and reprisals with the simple gift of worship. For worship is not a task, not a work, not something we achieve. It is not the result of our songs and prayers succeeding in pleasing a hard-to-please God. We are not the subject, the focus; it is not about us. It does not depend upon doing the right things in the right way, or singing only anointed songs, or any other human ordinance we might come up with. Let's go back to that verse in Hebrews, where the writer himself takes us back to Psalm 22 in order to understand what Jesus is doing on the cross. Calvin comments on this verse that 'Christ leads our songs and is the chief composer of our hymns',[9] and again, 'Christ

9. Quoted in C. Cocksworth, *Holy Holy Holy*, p. 159.

is the great choirmaster who tunes our hearts to sing God's praise.'[10]

> The fact that Jesus Christ is the leader of our worship, the high priest who forgives us our sins and leads us into the holy presence of the Father, is the central theme of the Epistle to the Hebrews . . . [it] contrasts two forms of worship: true worship which means reposing on and participating in the self offering of Christ who alone can lead us into the . . . holy presence of the Father – and false worship with its false reliance on what we do by following our own devices or the traditions of men . . . Worship is an ordinance of grace.[11]

That is to say, worship is a gift! Jesus has done it all! All we do is hold out our hands and say, 'Thank you, Jesus!'

Anything else keeps us locked in the dark days of life before the cross, where we could try hard to worship God appropriately and fail. Every time. Because the weight of sin – the legacy of a world filled with wrong worship, inadequate worship, false worship, the worship of evil and anything but God – won every time. Until Jesus. Until the cross. And now we can be infected by this perfect worship. We can catch it as easily as we can catch a common cold (only with far better consequences). It is the gift of God, this life of worship, this

---

10. Quoted in J. B. Torrance, *Worship, Community and the Triune God*, Preface.
11. *Ibid.*, pp. 47–50.

new creation, this eternal song of praise. Jesus has done it, and he has done it for us. What we now do is a participation in the worship of Jesus through the power of the Holy Spirit. A participation in his obedience, his self-giving, his communion with the Father, his purity, his words and his deeds. It's not the same as his worship because we are not the same. He was perfect and we need to be forgiven. He is God and we are his people. We deserve nothing and are given everything – treated as sons and heirs, filled with the same Spirit, loved with the same love. Jesus' worship is our salvation event; our worship is a celebratory riding on his coat tails, holding his hands, singing his songs, living his life.

Matthew records Jesus appearing on only two occasions after the resurrection. Both times, those who see him fall in worship (Matthew 28:9,17). They get the point. They catch the worship bug off Jesus. It is contagious. Chris Cocksworth describes it this way:

> Jesus not only brought people into the presence of God and enabled them to worship, he was the one in whom God was experienced and through whom worship was offered. Hence they worshipped him. They knew that in Christ they were dealing with God, so they bowed down before him.[12]

The two women who had sat and watched Joseph of Arimathea put the body of Jesus in the tomb return to

---

12. C. Cocksworth, *Holy Holy Holy*, p. 72.

the scene. Only now an angel speaks to them: 'Jesus is risen; he is not here. Look, I've rolled the stone back from the entrance so you can see he is not here. Go, tell the others, and you will see Jesus in Galilee.' The women run, not daring to say a word to this figure like lightning, with shockingly white robes. They run to tell the disciples this confusing but exciting news, when suddenly they are brought up short. Jesus himself stands before them. 'Hello,' he says, as you would, and the women have no doubt that it is him. And in the early morning light they have one reaction: they fall to the floor, clasp his feet, coming towards to kiss them, worshipping Jesus.[13] Moments before they were filled with fear, but now faith rises. Jesus' words, 'Don't be afraid', are both necessary and superfluous. What is happening? How can this be? A million questions half-form themselves in the minds of the two amazed Marys, but also, in his presence, next to him, with him, there is such comfort, such sweetness, such power and love and such an urge to worship that fear is banished by simply being with him. Jesus repeats the angel's message, 'Go tell my dear brothers, and I'll see you in Galilee.' Brothers. They don't know it yet, but Jesus has won them the right to be called children of God, heirs of the family firm, joining in his own business of worshipping the Father. Full membership of the family of God. A gift for you, my brothers and sisters.

The soldiers tell the elders and chief priests tales of

---

13. Matthew 28:9, *prosekunesan* – 'they worshipped'.

earthquakes and angels and the stone being moved away as they lay terrified. And those who choose not to walk in the way of worship Jesus has opened up, carry on in their old lives; everything is new except to those who will only keep the old ways. They will not receive the gift of worship, so they must perforce carry on doing all their old deeds: a cover-up, lies to the governor, bribes for silence and compliance. Little sins that come straight from the main one; small moral transgressions arising out of failure to worship God in spirit and in truth. The worship choice makes the moral choice: these guys have made their own bed of wrong worship, now they lie in it.

Meanwhile, the eleven go to a mountain in Galilee, the place Jesus told them. Again as they see him, worship overwhelms them. They come towards to kiss the Son of God, bowing before him in humble adoration.[14] As Matthew's Gospel began with wise men worshipping Jesus, so it ends. We don't know how many wise men came to see the infant Jesus at the house in Bethlehem, but there are eleven of them here on the mountain in Galilee. The text says, 'They worshipped him; but some doubted.' Did some not get it? Is Matthew allowing for doubt in the place of worship? What is going on here?

The man these guys had spent three years with has just been crucified and turns up as the Son of God, victorious over sin and death, and the worship that he

---

14. Matthew 28:17, *prosekunesan* – 'they worshipped'.

offers his Father infects them and they find themselves on their knees. I think they are allowed a moment to say to themselves, 'What is going on here?' We can look at it calmly, study the events, think and pray our way through. These guys were just caught up in it, and if their heads and hearts were travelling at different speeds through the experience, who can blame them? But Jesus has the answer. And he does not negate their doubt, or tell them off for it. He allows their doubt in this place of worship, and then he speaks to it, answering his disciples' doubt with God's truth. As the eleven worship Jesus, they hear him speak, and everything is made clear.

It is as though he says, 'I know what you are thinking. I know this is all very new. But listen, for I am Lord. All authority in heaven and on earth has been given to me. This is the power of God and now it is mine. So go and make disciples, lots of them, everywhere you go, bringing others into this place of worship, this right relationship with their God – Father, Son and Holy Spirit – teaching them what I am like, and what that means they must do. This is the way God intervenes in life – the way I intervene – calling many to come and join us, to leave their lives of sin, to simply bow in obedience to God and watch what happens; and I am doing it through you. Yes, I am Lord. Here is power, here is intervention and here is my character, for you will never be alone. I will always be with you, till this world and all its sin is finally ended and the new heaven and the new earth fill the people of God with everlasting joy.'

As they worship Jesus on the mountain, their lives are changed for good. This worship is going to transform everything. Normal Galilean family life, a job – a wife, kids, holidays to Jerusalem – all flies out of the window. Worshipping Jesus rewrites the days of their lives. They have a new song to sing, a new life to lead. This worship has changed them for good. And the act of worship is followed by the command to do something: live it out. Worship with hearts and lips, and lives and deeds. Love God, love your neighbour. Worship Jesus, preach the gospel. Matthew reminds his church at the end of his story of the truths he told them at the beginning: this Christian life is about one thing and one thing only. There are lots of stories to remember, lots of lessons to be taken on board, lots of truth to learn, but one essential story, one essential truth, one essential lesson: worship God. That's the big picture. The rest will follow.

Imagine for a moment being in Matthew's church 30 years on from these events. Imagine hearing him read this stuff to you. Imagine the tremor in his voice and the stillness in the room as he repeats the story one more time. You can see the script in his hand, but you can also read the truth of it in his life, in the lines on his face, the light in his eyes, the deeds of his life, the invitation that brought you to this room. This man met Jesus after he died on a mountain in Galilee and worshipped the worshipping Son of God. He caught eternal life that day. You can sense a little touch of heaven floating around the room, the kingdom of God breaking out afresh, as his story of worship and what worship does to a person works its way into your own heart and begins to take hold there.

As it takes hold, something strange happens. Fears about the ordinary matters of everyday living – fears about your wife really loving you, your children's health, the security of your job, where the money will come from to pay the bills – hear the whisper of the voice of Jesus. 'Don't be frightened,' he says, and you'd love not to be frightened, but you don't know how. What if you are just deluding yourself? And you realise that your eyes have now looked back inwards again, so you look back at dear old Matthew, sitting there, his eyes closed, still unable to follow those final words of Jesus with anything but awed silence. And you imagine that younger Matthew, sitting at his tax collector's booth as Jesus passes by and says, 'Follow me.' You see him welcome the Lord into his house, and you hear again the scorn of the Pharisees as Jesus eats with 'sinners', and Jesus' gentle response: sick people need a doctor. You see him run away with the rest that dark Friday, and then gather with them again on the mountain in Galilee. You see him play his part on that first Pentecost morning, filled with God's power, and you see him proclaim his faith, his Lord, his God. You see him watch as his friends are murdered and scattered for the words they speak about Jesus; you see him walk out of Jerusalem for the final time. You see the pain of age and its wisdom. But most of all, you see a man infected with the Son's worship of the Father, a life transformed by the life of the Son of God, a man who knows what is important. And you smile as again his frail voice starts the inevitable song of praise. Always the same song: 'I will declare your name to my brothers; in the congregation I will praise you . . . proclaim his righteousness to a people yet unborn, for he has done it.'

Now there is a catch in your throat, a tear in your eye, a sudden understanding in your mind, and with all your heart you join the worship. You too bow down before Jesus. Matthew's voice unlocks your heart. You see the big picture; you sing salvation's song; you worship God.

Appendix: The Worship Word

I recently watched a courtroom drama on TV, where the prosecuting lawyer hounded the defence's main witness, asking again and again, 'Did you really see this man at this time? Are you sure?' Eventually, the simple process of questioning allowed a smidgen of doubt to appear in the witness's mind, and the whole case turned on this crucial moment.

Clearly, my whole argument in the second half of this book hinged on the word *proskuneo* in Matthew's Gospel, and on being really sure what it means. This appendix is here to fill in some of the background to the word, to make certain that I am being true to the text of the Bible.

The New Testament uses several words for 'worship',[1]

---

1. *threskia* – used 5 times in the NT; *sebo* – used (with derivatives) 15 times in the NT; *latreuo* – used (with derivatives) 26 times in the NT; *proskuneo* – used (with derivatives) 60 times in the NT.

but this one beats all the others added together for frequency of use, and Matthew uses it almost exclusively as he talks about this issue.[2]

The word itself is two words joined together: *pros*, meaning 'movement towards', and *kuneo*, which means 'I kiss'. Together the literal sense is 'I come towards to kiss'. This is not, however, a word a Greek Mills & Boon author would have used. The kiss in question would be a formal kiss – the way in medieval England a slave might kiss the hand of his or her master as a sign of loyalty or obedience. It does imply physical closeness, in that you have to be next to your master to do this, but it does not imply emotional closeness. The slave is lesser, the master greater. They are not equals, and this is no romantic tryst.

This sense of a lesser person acknowledging a greater leads to the idea that has come to be used in translating it of bowing down before someone. The sense of touch in the kiss is gone, but the sense of reverence, of knowing that this person is greater, remains. Indeed, my NIV Bible translates the word mainly as 'worship', but sometimes substitutes the idea of 'bowing down' instead. Most modern translations follow the same pattern.

To catch the full weight of what is going on when the New Testament, and particularly Matthew, uses this word, we have to see first of all how those who lived earlier used the word. This means we have to look

---

2. The one exception is *sebo* in Matthew 15:9.

at the Old Testament precedents, and only then at how Matthew fits it into the general New Testament picture.

Proskuneo in the Old Testament

Now whereas the New Testament was written in Greek, the Old Testament was not – at least, not originally. But by the time of Jesus, the Greek language was so common that many Jews used a Greek translation, rather than the original Hebrew and Aramaic. The version they used is called the Septuagint, first written in the third century BC, and in it the word *proskuneo* is used 176 times, mostly for the Hebrew word *shachah*. This was the word for divine worship, which also carries the concept of bowing down before someone you consider to be greater than you.

For example, in Exodus 24:1, God commands the leaders Moses had appointed over Israel, 'You are to *worship* at a distance.' The Hebrew word for 'worship' is *shachah*; the Greek in the Septuagint, *proskuneo*. Then, in Deuteronomy 26:10, Moses is telling the people how to make the offering of Firstfruits. He says, 'Place the basket before the Lord your God and *bow down* before him.' The Hebrew for 'bow down' is *shachah*, and in the Septuagint, sure enough, we find *proskuneo*. Although different English words are used in the NIV, the meaning is the same. It's all about worship. Right worship, where we acknowledge that God and God alone is greater than we are; that he has our obedience, and we will bow down and follow him. *Proskuneo* is used in the Greek version of the Old Testament because it carries both the bowing down and the worship meanings.

So why do the translators confuse the issue by sometimes using 'worship', while at other times making do with 'bow down'? Why not stick with 'worship' all the time? The answer is partly that from time to time the Hebrew uses several different words for worship in a row (e.g. Deuteronomy 8:19 – 'If you ever . . . follow other gods and worship and bow down to them'), and then the sense demands some explanation. You might scratch your head and wonder what the translator was on if that verse I just quoted read, 'If you ever . . . worship other gods and worship and worship them'!

But another reason for varying the translation comes because actually *proskuneo* in the Septuagint is not only used of worship of God or false gods, but sometimes, like the Hebrew *shachah*, it describes how people behave towards other people. For example, in the story of the young Joseph's dreams in Genesis 37. When the corn sheaves bow to Joseph, and when the sun, moon and stars do the same, that bowing down is done with the *proskuneo* word. Moses bows down to his father-in-law Jethro with this word in Exodus 18:7. David bows down before King Saul in 1 Samuel 24:8, Saul before the prophet Samuel in 1 Samuel 28:14. The lovely Bathsheba does it to King David in 1 Kings 1:16. His resident palace prophet Nathan subsequently repeats that action in 1 Kings 1:23, and the band of travelling prophets bow to Elisha as he steps into his master

Elijah's shoes in 2 Kings 2:15. *Proskuneo*, which we thought was about worship, is used for each of these occasions.

We need to be careful here, because I build an argument from the Gospel of Matthew, where this word *proskuneo* is important, so we have to see for sure that, by the time Matthew wrote, the word was clearly understood as meaning worship, and only worship. After all, in Chapter 3 we looked at the word 'Lord' and saw that words matter, that words have meanings, and that understanding those meanings makes a difference to the way we act. We need to be sure what Matthew wants us to understand by this word. Does *proskuneo* in the New Testament mean the same as it does in the Old Testament? Does it still mean 'to show reverence generally; to bow down to anyone or anything you think greater than you', or has it come to mean 'to worship God' only?

Putting to one side the way the word is used in the book of Genesis, right at the beginning of the Bible, and in the life of David, the ideal king, *proskuneo* is used to mean bowing down to people fewer than 20 times in the rest of the history of Israel, the Psalms and the prophets. Of these, 15 come before the sacking of Jerusalem in 587 BC. That leaves four times that the word *proskuneo* is used to describe people bowing to other people in what might be referred to as the second half of the Old Testament.

This seems to indicate a shift in meaning, given that the word is still at this time regularly used to mean worship of God. At one time it was used of people, but gradually there is a change. This shift is even more noticeable when we see exactly what these four late stories are. Nebuchadnezzar 'falls prostrate before' Daniel after he explains his dream in Daniel 2:46, and then exclaims not praise or honour to Daniel but to God: 'Surely your God is the God of gods!' The other references come with Mordecai the Jew refusing to join others in 'bowing' to Haman in Esther 3, because such an action would be wrong. Are the people being required simply to honour Haman or to worship him? Either way, Mordecai won't risk it; he won't join in with everyone else. By this time, the word seems to mean worship much more often than not, even tending towards always meaning worship. This is not the way the word was used to describe Bathsheba simply greeting David, or the brothers merely bowing to Joseph. It may be used for worshipping the wrong things as well as the right things, but it does mean worship, not just respect and honour.

'Come towards to kiss'? Yes, but to kiss the divine, not any other earthly person, no matter how honourable. At one time it was used freely of God's king or messenger or people or prophet, but gradually it seems the word came to be increasingly the sole preserve of God himself. It was more and more for God, and God alone. This trend becomes complete in the New Testament.

Proskuneo in the New Testament

In the New Testament, *proskuneo* completes its journey and is clearly no longer applied to people: it becomes just for God. It's not for us to enjoy, but rather it is due to God, and God alone. When people try to apply this word to other people, they are stopped. This actually happens three times.

The first occasion is in Acts 10. Cornelius, a centurion in the Italian regiment, has a vision. An angel appears to him, commends his godly life, and tells him to send for Simon Peter who is visiting in Joppa. Peter, meanwhile, has a vision in which God tells him not to regard anyone as impure. The centurion's servants arrive, and Peter goes with them, because although as a Jew he should not enter their gentile master's house, he sees from his vision that God is at work. When he gets to the house, Cornelius 'met him and fell at his feet in reverence' (that's our worship word, right there). Peter replies immediately and in no uncertain terms, saying: 'Stand up . . . I am only a man myself' (Acts 10:25–26). What's the fuss, Peter? It's only a good man showing due reverence to a servant of God. Oh no it's not. Luke, in telling us this story, makes a simple point clearly: this reverence, this bowing before, this coming towards to kiss Peter's feet, is worship, acknowledging one greater than yourself, and it is wrong. Wrong when applied to another human being, that is. Right when applied to God. 'I'm only a man,' says Peter. Credit where credit is due, and that credit is God's, not Peter's.

The other two occasions when something like this happens are both at the end of the book of Revelation, in chapters 19 and 22. Think what it must have been like for John to see all the visions he records in his book. He has seen the glories of heaven, the throne of God, the Lamb slain but reigning in victory; the forces of the devil ranged against the people of God, but the people of God triumphant through the Spirit of God. It has been one enormous spiritual roller-coaster ride. And now at the end, as final victory is revealed, it all gets a bit much. The chap is overcome, and twice he falls to his knees to worship the angel who has shown him all these things, to kiss the bearer of such visions, such glory. Twice the angel replies in the same words: 'Do not do it! I am a fellow-servant with you and with your brothers who hold to the testimony of Jesus. Worship God!' (Revelation 19:10).[3] In Genesis 19:1 Lot 'bows down' (same word) to two angels and receives no reproof for his action. But times change, words develop, and now this word *proskuneo* is for God only. 'Don't do it to a man,' says Peter in Acts 10, and 'Don't even do it to angels' says Revelation 19 and 22: worship only God. A simple act with only one correct application. One rightful recipient. One God.

---

3. Revelation 22:9 has '. . . fellow-servant with you and with your
   brothers the prophets and of all who keep the words of this book.
   Worship God!'

Proskuneo in Matthew's Gospel

The reason all this is important is that Matthew uses this word *proskuneo* more than any other book in the New Testament, apart from Revelation, and he is telling us very clearly through it that Jesus is God, one who is rightly to be worshipped, not just revered. Matthew lives in the same world as fellow writers Luke and John. He knows what this word means. He knows it is for God alone, and yet he constantly uses it of people's reactions to Jesus.

We have taken the time to study this carefully because most contemporary versions of the Bible opt for a variety of translations of this word. Of the ten stories in the Gospel of Matthew that involve *proskuneo* worship, you would only find five if all you had in front of you was an English concordance and you used that to look up the word 'worship'. The others are translated as 'bow before', 'kneel before' and 'fall prostrate before'. Unless of course you still use the old King James Version, which unfailingly and consistently translates *proskuneo* as 'worship' every time. Actually, I'm not normally a fan of the King James Bible, with all its archaic language: 'faith, hope and charity' and so on. Charity – there you go, there's another word that has changed meaning. The King James translators didn't have a mental picture of Oxfam shops or people shaking tins in the shopping centre when they used that word. But we do. 'Faith, hope and love' is so much more easily understood. Yet here on this worship word the old Authorised Version is spot on, and my favourite

NIV doesn't quite match it. And I don't know why our modern translators make this choice, but I do know the effect of it.

I have two friends called James, and they have quite a lot in common: they are both tall, both in their twenties, both musical, both Christian, and they both worked as lay assistants in churches after they finished their degrees. But one of them loves the song 'Windmills of your mind' from the film *The Thomas Crown Affair*, and the other hates it. Its wistful melody, its bizarre imagery ('Like a circle in a spiral, like a wheel within a wheel', it always reminds me of the prophet Ezekiel) – one adores it, the other can't abide it. The very title of the song is enough to think about for quite a while. An unusual choice of words – I don't normally think of my mind as having windmills. I guess it refers to the way we sometimes endlessly turn the same things over again and again in our heads, particularly in the middle of the night, when something or someone or some idea or worry has taken hold and will not let go. It's an odd image, but that oddity stands out and produces these different reactions in the two James.

Likewise, I think Matthew wants us to see clearly the strangeness in the way people worship Jesus. I think he wants us to sit up straight and take note when he uses these worship stories. He wants us to be like the two James: to be taken aback by his imagery, to react strongly to what he is doing. Let me show you how this works in his Gospel. Read this first:

> While he was saying this, a ruler came and knelt before him
> and said, 'My daughter has just died. But come and put
> your hand on her, and she will live.' Jesus got up and went
> with him, and so did his disciples. (Matthew 9:18–19)

I dealt with the detail of this earlier, so for now the only
point I want to make is that if we go with the obvious
translation of *proskuneo* in this story, rather than the
version the NIV uses, the whole dynamic alters, and
Matthew is painting quite a different scene. Here it is
again, but this time I have changed one phrase to
capture what I believe Matthew wants us to see here:

> While he was speaking, a ruler came and worshipped him
> and said, 'My daughter has just died. But come and put
> your hand on her, and she will live.' Jesus got up and went
> with him, and so did his disciples.

This poor grieving father, a ruler of the synagogue no
less, worships Jesus and then makes his request. It's
quite a different picture than him just kneeling before
Jesus, isn't it? I mean, did he really *worship* Jesus? A
synagogue ruler worship another person? Given the
way no one seemed to listen to Jesus' predictions about
his death and resurrection, did they really have the
foggiest idea at this point that he was more than a
prophet, more than a potential Jewish king, more than
any other man? What is Matthew doing using this word
like this? It all seems very odd.

Matthew is making a point. A point about worship,
and how worshipping Jesus makes a huge difference to

us. It's supposed to be shocking – this Gospel is offen-
sive to people in Jesus' day, to Jews who see this kind of
action as simple blasphemy. Worship a man? Yes,
absolutely. But a man who happens to be God. And we
should peel back the interpretations of time and simply
see what we are meant to see. Matthew wants us to see
that people really did do this, in Jesus' lifetime, and that
it changed them.

Even if we accept that those who worshipped Jesus in
this way would not have put it in so many words right
there and then, and they might not have articulated the
truth behind the action in this way, we are left with
the fact that Matthew saw what happened, and as he
thought about it afterwards, he understood that
worship was happening here. Real worship. Worship
that made a difference.

Let me put it another way. If *proskuneo* is going to
mean anything other than worship in Matthew's
Gospel, if it is truly to be rendered simply as 'bow down
before' we have to have very good reasons for making
this call. 'Worship' is the main meaning of the word:
throughout the Old Testament, 121 times it clearly
means 'worship', against 55 times where it clearly means
'bow down before'. But this pales into insignificance
when we look at the New Testament record, where 55
times it clearly means 'worship',[4] against only a maxi-

---

4. Though it is not always translated so clearly: Acts 10:25 has 'fell at
his feet in reverence', though nobody is arguing this was an act of
worship which, as we have already seen, Peter rejects.

mum of five questionable 'bow down before' references. And those five are all in Matthew. In each of those five cases, Mark carries the same story with perfectly good words for 'bow down before'[5] – which Matthew sees fit to change. At the very least we must say that *proskuneo* carries both meanings, the physical act of bowing down before and the heart attitude of worship. It cannot be simply the former.

---

5. Mark 1:40 *gonypetōn*, falling on his knees; or Mark 5:22 *piptei pros tous podas autou*, he falls at his feet.

Other Survivor books include . . .

Red Moon Rising by **Pete Greig** – 24-7 is at the centre of a prayer revival across the globe and this book gives a fantastic insight into what God is doing with ordinary prayer warriors.

Passion for Your Name by **Tim Hughes** – To read this book is to share in a journey of discovery, of truths encountered, principles gleaned, mistakes made and lessons learned. A valuable companion for all worshippers!

The Truth Shall Set You Free by **Beth Redman** – This book is unashamedly about God, His heart for us, His love and mercy shown to us, and His promises made to us. It's the truth of knowing God that will heal us and ultimately bring contentment and peace to our lives.

Diary of a Dangerous Vision by **Andy Hawthorne** – The exciting story of the Message combined with crucial reflections and biblical teaching to equip you to run the race.

The Heart of Worship Files by **Matt Redman** – This book features highlights from the very popular website, heartofworship.com. Compiled by Matt Redman, it will encourage and inspire you to help others reach new depths of worship.

survivor

The Unquenchable Worshipper
by Matt Redman

This book is about a kind of worshipper. Unquenchable. Undivided. Unpredictable. On a quest to bring glory and pleasure to God, these worshippers will not allow themselves to be distracted or defeated. They long for their hearts, lives and songs to be the kind of offerings God is looking for.

'This is unashamedly a book about God and living a devoted life in His presence. Worship is about God, to God and for God. The Unquenchable Worshipper *shouts this truth out loud.'* (Mike Pilavachi, Soul Survivor)

Wasteland?
by Mike Pilavachi

Are you looking for greater depth in your Christian life? Tired of the consumer model of spirituality? Are you ready to do the *right* things, even when things are going *wrong*? Feel like investing in obscurity . . . ? Mountain tops can be invigorating, but there's growth in the valleys. God says, 'Meet me in the desert.'

'Mike Pilavachi draws on his own experience and the Bible to infuse faith, hope and love in us, and to inspire us on our journey.' (J. John, Philo Trust)

survivor